COLORADO MEMORIES
OF THE
NARROW GAUGE CIRCLE

by John Krause and Ross Grenard

ISBN 911868-59-3

Second printing May 1988

Front cover: In October 1957, Hal Carstens caught this Rio Grande narrow gauge scene at Alamosa, Colorado, when it was still a bustling dual gauge railroad town with through freight service to Durango and Silverton. Shot with ASA 12 Kodachome, Exakta camera.

Title Page: The engine crew was oblivious to Philip Hasting' camera as they concentrated on watering venerable Consolidation No. 278 at Jack's cabin on the Crested Butte branch a short time before abandonment. More photos of this locale appear on pages 36 and 37.

Inside Front Cover: Memorial Day, 1947 fan trip over the Rio Grande Southern was covered by many notable railfans. Philip A. Ronfor caught Mac Poor in this photo of the special.

Carstens
PUBLICATIONS, INC.

FREDON-SPRINGDALE ROAD FREDON TOWNSHIP
P O BOX 700, NEWTON N J 07860

An Introduction to the Narrow Gauge

"My end shall be my beginning" read the motto of Mary, Queen of Scots, and it is as applicable to the 675 miles of narrow gauge track that once served southwestern Colorado as it was to that tragic monarch. For the narrow gauge rails formed a circle extending from Salida and Alamosa on the east to Durango and Montrose on the west, with the 163 mile Rio Grande Southern forming the final link in the circle. Branches radiated to Ouray, Silverton, and Farmington, N. M.; up the San Luis valley, to the coal mines north of Gunnison, and to the limestone quarries atop Monarch Pass. Operating in an area where the minimum elevation was over 6,000 ft. and encompassing a plurality of Colorado's 14,000 ft. peaks, it served places whose incomparable scenic beauty, vast mineral resources, and scant population created a setting unmatched on the North American continent and whose names even today connote the glories of both railroading and mining.

The narrow gauge circle physically comprised those lines of the Denver and Rio Grande left untouched in the great changeover precipitated by the construction of the standard gauge Colorado Midland in the 1880's. Since the Denver-Ogden line was standard gauged in 1890, less than a year before the RGS drove its last spike the circle could probably be considered obsolescent even at its birth. Those were prosperous years, but the repeal of the Sherman Silver Purchase Act and the subsequent Panic of 1893 marked the beginning of a static economy for southwest Colorado that would generate precious little rail traffic growth in the century to come.

Control of the RGS passed to the Grande in the 1895 reorganization and it was operated as a part of the larger system until 1929. After the turn of the century, the Rio Grande itself was consolidated managerially with the Missouri Pacific to the east and the Western Pacific to the west as a portion of George Gould's ill-fated transcontinental system. The narrow gauge was left largely intact and to a certain extent ignored save as a feeder line for the Missouri Pacific. It was to remain peripheral to the energies expended in the gathering conflict as Gould relentlessly poured the resources of his railroads into such efforts as the Western Pacific and the Wabash-Pittsburgh Terminal.

One result of the Gould control, particularly after the completion of the Western Pacific, was a concerted effort to lure transcontinental passengers away from the established Union Pacific and Santa Fe routes and Maj. Shadrack K. Hooper was entrusted with the task of marketing Colorado to the travelling public. One of his more successful efforts was the Narrow Gauge Circle, a four day tour starting in either Alamosa or Salida and offering a ride around the narrow gauge by daylight to view the wonders of Marshall Pass, the Black Cañon, Lizard Head and the trestles of Ophir, plus such options as the Silverton Branch and a stage ride over the Red Mountain. Offered as either a side trip on transcontinental tickets or as a separate tour out of Denver, the summer only jaunt was well received and was a staple of Rio Grande passenger promotions until 1926. In that year the Curecanti Needle disappeared from the D&RGW herald to be replaced by the phrase "Royal Gorge Route", and although passenger service still operated over most of the narrow gauge lines, the efforts of the Rio Grande's passenger department would be more and more devoted to the standard gauge operations. The year 1926 was also significant for it marked the beginnings of what was to become Rio Grande Motorway, with bus and truck operating rights paralleling most of the railroad, and the later stated intent of its president "to substitute highway service on branch lines operating at a substantial loss". This, of course, meant primarily the narrow gauge.

In 1929 the circle was severed for the first time when the Ames mud slide on the RGS between Vance Junction and Ophir neatly split that unfortunate carrier in twain. Since the RGS' operating costs now equalled 125% of its total revenues, the Rio Grande wanted out. President J.S. Pyeatt declared that clearing the slide would cost over $30,000 and could not be justified under existing conditions. A bankruptcy petition was instituted by the bondholders and Denver businessman Victor Miller was appointed receiver by the U.S. District Court in Denver. Miller succeeded in clearing the slide for $500 and went on to take other measures that insured the railroad's improbable existence for at least two more decades. Most notable among these was the replacement of the steam powered mixed trains with converted Buick and Pierce-Arrow motors that were to be known in legend as the Galloping Geese. These very effectively cut costs, improved service, and

helped maintain the vital mail contract. Miller also began returning leased Rio Grande engines, performing shop work at Ridgway instead of having the Grande do the work at Alamosa. He also purchased freight cars and cut costs while otherwise improving service. His tenure ended in 1938 but he brought to the Rio Grande Southern a glimmer of its old spirit and vitality at its darkest hour since 1893.

Much has been written of the glory years of passenger service in the 1920's, but it is doubtful that there was much spillover to the narrow gauge as the equipment had been purchased in the 1880's and precious little modernization has occurred. Open platform coaches with kerosene lamps and leather or plush walkover seats were still the rule, and coal stoves provided heat. Food service was accomplished at 20 minute meal stops at Chama, Sargent, Gunnison, and Cimarron. Parlor car service was offered on the Alamosa-Silverton and Salida-Ouray runs. During the summers an open top observation car was operated through the Black Cañon at a modest 25¢ additional charge.

The Rio Grande's bankruptcy in 1935 and the appointment of two local men, Wilson McCarthy and Henry Swan, as trustees to operate the property was to have far-reaching effect in the railroad world as the renascent carrier struggled for and finally attained its place in the sun. Vast amounts were spent on improving the railroad, particularly the old D&SL Moffat Tunnel line acquired the year before. Interestingly, one of the first rehabilitation programs involved the narrow gauge passenger car fleet. In 1937, some $100,000 was authorized to rebuild eight coaches, five parlor cars, several baggage cars, and upgrade at least 14 locomotives at Alamosa. The nineteenth century standards of open platforms, oil lights and coal stoves were replaced by modern appliances. Three of the parlor cars - *Alamosa*, *Durango*, and *Chama* - were equipped with stainless steel galleys and dinette sections and were staffed by a one-man crew who also served as an itinerant storekeeper, dispensing such amenities of civilization as ice cream cones, newspapers, thread, and other small items to the populace between Chama and Durango.

Despite the upgrading of the narrow gauge equipment, the passenger miles continued to decrease as bus service replaced first the branchline trains and then the Gunnison-Montrose and Montrose-Ouray trains in the mid-30's. The Depression saw branches abandoned and the remaining traffic snapped up by Rio Grande Motorway. In 1940, the *Shavano* was discontinued and regular passenger service over the old Marshall Pass mainline came to an end. The same year a petition was filed to abandon the famed Chili Line from Antonito to Santa Fe, N.M. The line was down to a mixed train handling an average of one car a day, yet in a foretaste of what was to come in the postwar years, the petition produced acrimonious proceedings before both the New Mexico state government and a Senate subcommittee before permission was obtained to drop the line. The last physical remnant of Col. Palmer's great plan for a railroad from Denver to El Paso passed into history on September 1, 1941. Ironically, the following year saw the building of Los Alamos, the "Atomic City", along the abandoned right-of-way of the Chili Line.

The Japanese attack on Pearl Harbor put a moratorium on service abandonments and brought about a revival of metal mining as foreign sources fell victim to the Axis rampage. Demand for lumber, meat, and foodstuffs soared and the narrow gauge became an important transportation artery as gasoline rationing was put in effect and tires disappeared from the shelves. The Army stepped in and drafted seven of the Sports Model 2-8-2's and a number of freight cars for use on the narrow gauge White Pass & Yukon in Alaska. The Office of Defense Transportation very nearly tore up the whole Rio Grande Southern for shipment to Alaska, but local citizens, aided by the late Congresswoman Elizabeth Pellet, obtained $65,000 in financing from the Defense Supplies Corporation to keep the RGS running. The government's sudden change of heart seemed odd at the time, but shortly afterward mining resumed near Placerville and the Durango smelter was leased by the U.S. Vanadium Company. Carloads of a seemingly worthless form of tailings called "yellow cake" rolled into Durango and then on to an Army plant in Utah. Not until August of 1945 did anyone realize that the valiant old RGS had been a part of the dawn of the nuclear age.

The end of World War II brought reorganization of the Rio Grande, the end of gas rationing and an expanded road building program in the territory served by the narrow gauge. In 1946 the RGS again tottered on the brink of abandonment and the Rio Grande Chief Engineer, Alfred E. Perlman (who is best remembered for his tenure as president of the ill-starred Penn Central), invited Lucius Beebe and Charles Clegg to accompany him on an inspection tour aboard the two remaining narrow gauge office cars, B-2 and B-7, on what was the first steam powered special to tour the entire RGS since Victor Miller had enter-

tained John Barriger in 1936. Thanks to Beebe's dispatches to the New York Herald-Tribune and the wire service pickups, the trip turned into a media event replete with champagne sipping, gourmet delicacies, and black tie dinners. All of this was described in Beebe's purple prose and probably brought the struggling line more publicity than anything since Otto Mears had splurged on silver passes.

Despite traffic losses, the RGS continued to operate. In 1947, a combination of declining business and a dirt slide of major proportions east of Cedar Creek caused the Rio Grande to petition for abandonment of the Sapinero-Cedar Creek segment of the old Marshall Pass mainline. Permission was granted in 1948, and in June of 1949, the rails were removed and the circle was broken for the first time. In August, petitions were filed with the ICC to abandon the Valley Line over Poncha Pass from Mears Junction to Hooper, followed the following month by a petition before the Colorado PUC to discontinue the *San Juan*. Opposition to both actions were unexpectedly strong, with many of the citizens of the area wondering whether the 1947 reorganization had merely exchanged one group of robber barons for another.

On the last day of January 1951, the *San Juan* passed into history, ending some 80 years of regular passenger service into the San Juan Basin. However, it was not the end of narrow gauge passenger service, for the New Mexico Corporation Commission refused to acquiesce in the Colorado decision and required operation of a daily train from Chama to Dulce until May 22nd when permission was resignedly granted to suspend the service. The abbreviated and short-lived *San Juan* was operated with Mikado No. 473 and a single combine pulled from the Silverton mixed.

February 15th of 1951 also saw the last run over the Valley Line and the two remaining segments of the narrow gauge circle were now torn asunder. Since the major use of the line in recent years had been to transfer equipment and locomotives back and forth to the shops at Alamosa, the abandonment precluded the operation of any more passenger trains over the trackage out of Salida. The Valley Line, known in the timetables as the Alamosa Branch, had been constructed in 1889 as an extension of the Mears Junction-Orient mine branch. It was principally noted for having the longest stretch of tangent track on the Rio Grande, some 53 miles of straight line from Villa Grove to Alamosa, and for offering a panoramic view of the Sangre de Cristo and Culebra ranges.

Nineteen forty nine also marked the year in which the RGS ceased to be an all weather carrier, following a boiler explosion which destroyed its rotary snow plow. At the same time, a deferral of maintainence in response to declining revenues had produced a situation in which derailments were commonplace, service lapses frequent, and in 1950, the Post Office cancelled the mail contract. This meant not only the end of passenger service, but also the loss of considerable revenue. At the same time, several of the major mines announced plans to begin shipping by truck or simply closed up shop as did at least one major lumber mill. Resourceful as ever, the Ridgway shops converted the Geese into a tourist configuration, seating some 24 people, and commenced offering tourist trips out of Ridgway, Durango, and Dolores. The service was popular and numerous trips operated in 1950 and 1951. Unfortunately by then the situation had become intolerable with unpaid bills, few revenues to meet them, and no predictable future sources of cash. The counties through which the railroad operated were demanding their back taxes with interest, Railroad Retirement contributions had not been paid, and in the fall of 1951, the Receiver applied for permission to abandon. This was granted by the ICC in 1952, and the circle's most glamorous component ended its precarious existence.

At about the same time as the scrappers commenced work on what was once Otto Mears' pride and joy, petitions were filed by the Rio Grande for abandonment of the Ouray and Cedar Creek lines, and following the closing of the mine at Crested Butte, for all of the remaining track west of Poncha Junction. Both petitions were granted and last runs occurred in 1953 and 1954 respectively. Since there was still some business at Ridgway, the line down from Montrose was standard gauged.

Thus at the end of 1954, a little over 300 narrow gauge miles remained, in two isolated and fairly busy segments: the 21 miles from Salida to Monarch, and the 290 miles from Alamosa to Silverton and Farmington. The isolated Monarch branch's *raison d'etre* was the limestone quarry at the end of the branch which supplied the flux for Colorado Fuel & Iron's Minnequa blast furnaces and justified twice-daily operations up the 4.5% grades and over the switchbacks at Garfield. In June of 1956, the branch was standard gauged and all the remaining equipment was transferred by standard gauge flat cars to Alamosa, thus ending some 90 years of narrow gauge operations.

During the early 1950's oil and gas were discovered in the Four Corners area and around Ignacio. The area experienced a boom of some proportions and the narrow gauge shared in it, handling pipe, cement, and other bulk items over the Cumbres Pass line. For several years almost daily operation was called for and together with the expansion of lumbering, the pipe trains probably saved the line from certain extinction. New cars were constructed, student firemen and brakemen were hired, and nearly all of the 480's and 490's were put in active service. By 1956 daily operations were commonplace and cost studies had been completed on the relative merits of converting the line to standard gauge vis-a-vis purchase of narrow-gauge diesels. Enginemen and conductors who remembered the days of diamond stacks and link and pin were sharing cab and caboose with firemen and brakemen not yet old enough to vote.

Unfortunately, in 1957 the traffic subsided and three-day-a-week operation became the rule, with coal, lumber, crude oil from a field north of Chama, and other commodoties not lending themselves to truck transport making up the body of the business. While the pipe traffic was sustaining the freight business of the railroad, the Silverton was handling an increasing number of passengers. By 1952, all of the line's coaches were in summer only service, and after the ore business from Silverton dried up in 1953, the 461 and 462 became almost 100% passenger during the summer months. One Rio Grande passenger official was quoted by the *Wall Street Journal* as declaring "we have a gold mine by the tail, and we don't know what to do with it". In 1954 abandonment was threatened and at least two groups offered plans for saving the line which engendered more controversy among the local population than anything else. In 1955, a truce of sorts was declared and the railroad shopped the equipment, painted all the coaches yellow, and placed the train on a daily schedule. In 1957 reclining seats in the vestibule coaches and swivel chairs in the surviving parlor car *Alamosa* were removed to increase seating capacity.

Unfortunately freight business continued to decline as the pipe business completely dried up and no new sources of traffic appeared. In 1964, the refinery at Alamosa closed and the crude oil business from Chama was no more. In December of that year, for the first time in history, no effort was made to open Cumbres Pass after the first snowfall and the line was closed until the spring of 1965, with all freight diverted to Rio Grande Motorway. By 1966 its physical condition had deteriorated so badly that the railroad refused to operate any more excursions. That year only 20 freights were operated west of Antonito and in 1967 application was filed to abandon the Alamosa-Farmington line, thus bringing to an end both 97 years of narrow gauge freight operations and not incidentally Class 1 steam freight operations in North America.

Let this volume serve as a tangible token not only to the days of our youth and its three foot Camelot, but of a world now passed with the snows of yesteryear. For once the San Juans and the other towering peaks looked down on a unique and unforgettable epoch in rail transportation; when smoke rose over the alpine meadows and the fingers of steel extended to their ultimate.

ACKNOWLEDGEMENTS: Robert A. LeMassena, A. Sheffer Lang, Robert W. Richardson, Donna McCulloch, and a host of employees of the Rio Grande and RGS who, in the days before the phrase "generation gap" made its appearance, were never hesitant to discuss their railroad with those who were quite a bit younger.

A Personal Introduction from John Krause

The combination of narrow gauge railroading and the scenic wonders of Colorado was as much as any railroad photographer could ask for. Those postwar years before the Narrow Gauge Circle was broken offered the visitor a look back in time at railroading much as it had been in the early part of the century. Colorado narrow gauge was an empire in itself with which modern times had not caught up, where steam power lasted right up until the last of the Circle was gone.

Colorado Memories takes the reader back in time for a scenic look at the Narrow Gauge Circle. Thanks to the efforts of eleven different photographers, your journey will cover over six hundred miles of narrow-gauge where you will discover the almost-forgotten fantrips and freights of yesteryear. Enjoy the ride on the passenger trains as they made their way over Cumbres and Marshall Passes and journey up the branch lines and through the Black Cañon on the last runs forever.

Your authors have made every effort to present photos that have never been published before. Thanks to the photographic efforts of people like Robert F. Collins, Bob Andrews, and Sam Fredricks — to name just a few — we were able to bring to light many new pictures to illustrate the famous Narrow Gauge Circle. While a few photos may have been in print before, we feel that this presentation of over 240 views presents a new and different look at railroading in Colorado.

Putting this book together was a pleasant trip back in time for me. Through the efforts of Ross Grenard and Ed Crist, together with hundreds of hours in the darkroom, the pictures were printed, the layout designed, and the writing done. My special thanks to everyone for their interest and help.

John Krause

Contents

Salida

Most trips around the Narrow Gauge Circle began at Salida, where the original narrow gauge mainline and the Tennesee Pass main diverged. Although overnight sleeper service out of Denver was available up to 1939, most chose to take an additional day and use the *Scenic Limited*, whose dining service, observation lounge, and daylight ride from Denver via the Royal Gorge made it one of the nation's premier trains.

RIGHT: On August 17, 1939, the *Scenic Limited* was all Pullman green, 14 cars long, and practically-new 4-8-4 No. 1800 provided the power. Here the big Baldwin slakes its thirst and gets a shot of Alemite in front of the old stone station before continuing up the 1.4% grade to Tennessee Pass and on to Grand Junction and Salt Lake City.

BELOW: Since the *Scenic Limited* arrived at 3:00 PM and the *Shavano* departed the next morning, Salida offered varied opportunities for train watching; even in 1952, when narrow-gauge Mikes, a 2-8-0 from the Gould era, and 1942-built FT's might be observed in concert. The purist might well have lamented the lack of an articulated, but on that rainy September 27th in 1952, who would know that all aspects of the scene, including Salida's status as a division point, were to pass from the scene in a comparatively short time?

Robert F. Collins

Philip R. Hastings

Salida's engine terminal serviced both the largest and smallest of the Rio Grande's steam locomotives. *ABOVE LEFT:* 4-8-4 No. 1801 and K-36 Mike No. 483 pause for a moment of contemplation. Both Baldwin graduates, class of 1937 and 1925 respectively, they represented the highest refinement of steam power on both the standard and narrow gauge lines.

BELOW RIGHT: The railroad facilities in Salida lay directly alongside the Arkansas River and after making a sharp curve, the narrow gauge crossed the river and headed south. On a rainy day in 1952, the 486 brought in a stock train across the bridge which had known the passage of so many narrow gauge trains.

BELOW LEFT: A little further on, the 483 on another day prepares to move its train of Monarch limestone down the main to the yard where it will be moved by a dual gauge switcher to the barrel transfer east of town for transshipment to the blast furnaces at Pueblo.

Philip R. Hastings

Philip R. Hastings

John L. Treen

Sam Fredericks

TOP LEFT: For a number of years, the Rio Grande's Monte Cristo Hotel and the morning train to Gunnison were integral parts of the Salida scene. In 1940, the *Shavano* departed from the scene and the hotel was torn down shortly after World War II, but in 1940, Sam Fredericks brought the town's namesake parlor car and the fascinating structure together. Since the parlor car boasted no dining facilities, it can be assumed that the passengers are breakfasting in the dining room.

BOTTOM: The Salida shop force took great pride in the engines assigned to them for service, and maintained them well both mechanically and in appearance. On September 19, 1949, they turned out Engine 499 for a Rocky Mountain Railroad Club special with silvered cylinder heads, Russia Iron (olive green) boiler jacket, aluminum striping, and polished rods. On that pleasant morn, the last built of all Rio Grande narrow gauge engines gets a final check as Tenderfoot Mountain looks down, and dual gauge switcher 1173 moves the train into the station.

Ross Grenard

9

Monarch Branch

What was to be the last narrow gauge passenger train out of Salida operated on May 24, 1950, when the 489 handled a Rocky Mountain Railroad Club special over the Monarch Branch and Poncha Pass Lines. *ABOVE LEFT:* Near the end of third rail, the 2-8-2 moved its six car train up the 2.3% grade out of the Arkansas Valley, following in the path of uncounted passenger trains, specials, and mixes that had rolled over the narrow gauge main since 1880.

BELOW LEFT: At Poncha Junction, the Monarch Branch diverged from the main line and headed up the narrowing valley of the South Branch of the Arkansas River. Though it had been without an operator for many years, the station stood solid up to the end of operations, and even after the abandonments of the early 1950's, witnessed the twice daily passage of the limestone trains. *BELOW RIGHT:* At Maysville wye, 6.9 miles west of Poncha Junction, the westbounds paused to set out half their cars in respect to both the 4.5% grades that lay ahead, and the limiting length of the trailing track at the Garfield switchback.

Ross Grenard

John L. Treen   John L. Treen

Ross Grenard

Above Maysville, a 24 degree double horseshoe curve, looping from one side of the valley to the other, was necessary to maintain even a 4.5% grade. On May 24, 1950, the assault on the grade was as spectacular as anything on the narrow gauge as the 489 brings the last passenger train up the grade and across U. S. 50.

Robert W. Andrews

Ross Grenard

At Silver Creek Tank, between Maysville and Garfield, stood the only watering facility on the branch. *LEFT:* After filling up its tank, the 499 started up and rolled across the timber trestle for the benefit of the photographers. The reservoir for the water column can be seen above the baggage car, a radical departure from the traditional wooden water tank. Garfield switchback was the limiting factor for train size on the branch, and its most spectacular feature. Its construction was mandated by the extreme narrowness of the valley which precluded another Maysville loop, and the necessity to maintain grade. *BELOW LEFT:* Standard operating procedure on both westbound and eastbound trains is illustrated by the 482 backing up the switchback with the first half of the train. At the upper switch, he will pull forward into the clear to await the arrival of the helper with the second section, then couple up and continue the remaining three miles to the quarry. *ABOVE RIGHT:* On downward trips, the helper, in this case 492, would run ahead of the train, wait in the clear at the upper end for the road engine to bring down the first cut, then grab on to the second cut, bring it down, set it on the second of two receiving tracks, and return to Maysville. After which the road engine would couple up and bring the train to Maysville. Since the lower switch at Garfield was located next to U. S. 50, watching the Monarch train's gyrations was a popular exercise for the tourist as well as the railfan. *BELOW:* The eastbound movement of the September, 1949 Railroad Club special down the switchback was an unusual sight even for the train watcher. Lack of turning facilities for the passenger train at Monarch caused the reverse operation of the consist that day.

Robert W. Andrews

Robert W. Andrews

LEFT: On May 23, 1949, the 492 added her 37,000 pounds of tractive effort to boosting an extra towards the 10,000 foot elevation of Monarch, as *Trains'* Associate Editors Strassman and Morgan enjoyed the view from an empty gondola car, in a scene typical of the upper part of the branch. *RIGHT:* With clear stack and popping safety valve, the 489 brings the last passenger train ever to traverse the line into Monarch, past the piles of limestone, the outfit cars which housed the carmen assigned to inspect cars before they began the descent, and the general company town atmosphere. Spring comes very late at this altitude, but the sun is bright on the scene. Two 1953 scenes illustrate the normal pattern of rail operations at Monarch and the nature of the quarry. *BELOW LEFT:* 482 backs around the wye, and *BELOW RIGHT:* 483 makes up the train for Salida. Such operations were generally handled with the precision of a ballet, for the 8 mph speed restriction on eastbound trains and retainers turned to the 20 lb. position often caused the down grade trips to take considerably longer than coming up hill. The line from Salida to Poncha Junction and up to Monarch mine remains a principal source of limestone for the Colorade Fuel & Iron Company's blast furnaces at Pueblo. Standard gauged in 1956, the dynamic brakes on today's GP9's and contemporary air brake systems have eliminated much of the drama of the ascent and descent.

Poncha Junction to Mears Junction

LEFT: The 499 was heading an Alamosa-bound freight on March 17th, 1950, as it rolled empty stock cars through Poncha Junction. No operator was on hand, as the station had long since been converted to maintenance-of-way use, but in that year trains for Gunnison, Alamosa, and Monarch still passed by its doors. RIGHT: Just west of Poncha, the main line turned south and began its climb up the 4% to Poncha and Marshall Passes. On May 25, 1950, the 490, assisted by the 489, headed up the grade in a view which shows both the area around Poncha Junction and, dimly in the haze, Mt. Princeton.

FAR RIGHT: Climbing out of Poncha Junction, the 489 passes through the first of several cuts near Otto on the way to Mears Junction. In the background below can be glimpsed the panorama of the Arkansas Valley and the Collegiate range which dominates the area. Although the grade is a steady 4%, the tough little Baldwin Mike is making light work of its six car passenger train.

Robert W. Andrews

Robert F. Collins

Robert W. Andrews

John Krause

LEFT: Returning to Salida from the last excursion over Poncha Pass, the 489 is trailed by the now familiar motorcade on Highway 160. Note the 1940 LaSalle leading the pack.

BELOW: The traces of a late spring snowstorm are still apparent as the 489 appears again on a more melancholy occasion, heading a scrap train across Silver Creek near Otto on the 4% grade in the spring of 1955. After climbing out of Poncha Junction, the line followed the creek valley west across the solidly constructed trestle and headed for Mears Junction.

Ross Grenard

Mears Junction and the Valley Line

Eleven miles west of Salida and 1400 feet higher, Mears Junction was the first of many water tanks on the narrow-gauge, and a set out point for freight moving from Gunnison to Alamosa. On September 19, 1949, the 499 drank deeply from the tank before moving up the 4% of Poncha Pass, and prepared for a photo run on the Valley Line bridge.

The track arrangement at Mears was an unusual one, and like no other on the Rio Grande narrow gauge as this series of pictures illustrates. *LEFT:* The 499 has switched off to its right and is starting up the Valley Line trackage. In the center may be seen the Marshall Pass Line, a weed grown storage track, and the Valley Line nearest to the camera, with the photographers standing on it. *BELOW:* A little further up the line, the train curves onto a 20 degree curved trestle to cross the main line. *RIGHT:* In the final scene, 499 curves around the trestle, crossing over the main and Silver Creek before heading for the summit some 3 miles further and 328 feet higher.

Robert F. Collins

Ross Grenard

Robert W. Andrews

Ross Grenard   Robert W. Andrews

The 9059 foot summit of Poncha Pass is not spectacular in terms of scenery, but it does possess a charm with Mt. Ouray looming in the background and a foliage pattern of sagebrush, pines, and aspen. Once the summit of Otto Mears' toll road from Saugache to the riches of Leadville, it is the divide between the Arkansas and Rio Grande River watersheds, and is one of those spots where history is always present. *LEFT:* The 499 handles a Rocky Mountain Railroad Club special in the fall of 1949, a few miles north of the Pass. *ABOVE LEFT:* The special pauses at the summit. *ABOVE:* The following spring, the 499 shows off her dual service capabilities as she brings a train of empty stock cars and Baldwin Branch coal down the 1.42% grade, south of Round Hill on the way to Alamosa.

RIGHT: The Villa Grove wye once extended some 8 miles further into the foothills of the Sangre de Cristo to serve the Orient Mine, whose iron ore deposits were the rationale for constructing the line in 1881. After the ore played out, the branch was abandoned in 1940, but the wye remained in 1950 to turn what was to be the last passenger train in the shadows of the Sangre de Cristo. *BELOW:* Villa Grove water tank was an unusual one; for its size, color, and nature departed sharply from the standard Rio Grande practice. After the Valley Line's demise, the tank was taken to Jack's Cabin on the Crested Butte Branch where it replaced another that had fallen into disrepair. *BELOW RIGHT:* The line south of Villa Grove to Alamosa was unique in that it consisted of 53 miles of tangent track through what was once a vast inland sea. Its construction in 1889 was motivated by the necessity to have a narrow gauge connection between the Marshall Pass line and the San Juan Extension, and a projected agricultural boom in the valley. The state of Mineral Hot Springs illustrates what happened to the traffic potential on the line, but its importance as a connection is illustrated as 499 heads south with empty stock cars for the Alamosa shop and some 12 cars of Baldwin Branch coal.

Robert W. Andrews

Ross Grenard

Robert W. Andrews

23

Marshall Pass Line

John Krause

Robert F. Collins

LEFT: On the way to Poncha Junction with a train of scrap rail, the 489 eases around the bottom of the loop at Shirley, some 2 miles out of Mears Junction. Such operations were an almost daily occurance during the summer of 1955, when the scrapping of the railroad resulted in more trips being made over Marshall than had been made for the last year of operation. Leased to the contractor, the Mike will deliver its cars to the Rio Grande at Poncha Junction, pick up empties, and then return over the one time Otto Mears toll road to continue the process. Soon the scrap train will reach the pass and after three quarters of a century of narrow gauge railroading, the 10,656 foot summit will be left to the mountains, the storms, and memories.

BELOW: On August 18, 1939, the 479 leads the *Shavano* around one of the 24 degree curves at Gray's Siding. Though the days of passenger service on Marshall Pass were numbered, the solid green consist was impressive as it rolled towards Gunnison on a peaceful summer morning. While 4% grades and 24 degree curves are hardly indicative of efficiency, the one time Otto Mears toll road bed, purchased by the Rio Grande, was an infinitely better crossing of the Continental Divide than that of the South Park at Alpine Pass. *RIGHT:* With Mt. Ouray in the background, and the timberline only a few feet above, the scrap train moves east to the water tank for a drink before tying up for the night. Soon twilight will fall, not only for the day but also for an era of railroading. But for the present, the loneliness of Marshall Pass will be broken by the sound of narrow gauge exhaust.

Marshall Pass lies between the summits of Mt. Ouray on the north and Chipeta on the south. Twenty-five miles west of Salida and 3,000 feet higher, the 10,586 foot summit boasted at one time the highest post office in the continental United States, and was a relatively self-contained community consisting of a telegraph office, boarding house, turntable, and passing track, all under the cover of the snowshed. This photo shows Marshall Pass looking south with the 489 emerging from the shed during scrapping operations.

LEFT: In September of 1954, the clean-up train stopped at the summit and for the last time turned up the retainers prior to descending the east slope. As the smoke filtered through the roof of the shed and the brakeman went about his duties for almost the last time, Mt. Ouray looked down majestically and eternally at the end of an era. *BELOW:* Another view from the east end of the snowshed, looking towards Mt. Ouray and down the east slope of the pass. *BELOW LEFT:* The telegraph office where brass pounders once practiced their skills had long since been closed when this somewhat ethereal study was made, showing the enclosed nature of the station at Marshall Pass, and evoking memories of the days when continuous operations were necessary and the wires carried the communications traffic of a transcontinental mainline. As Bob Richardson walks away, the crumbling structure is left to the elements, the scrappers, and history.

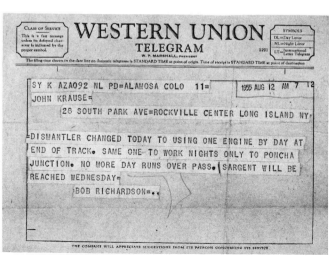

WESTERN UNION TELEGRAM

SY K AZA092 NL PD=ALAMOSA COLO 11=   1955 AUG 12 AM 7 12

JOHN KRAUSE=

28 SOUTH PARK AVE=ROCKVILLE CENTER LONG ISLAND NY=

DISMANTLER CHANGED TODAY TO USING ONE ENGINE BY DAY AT END OF TRACK. SAME ONE TO WORK NIGHTS ONLY TO PONCHA JUNCTION. NO MORE DAY RUNS OVER PASS. SARGENT WILL BE REACHED WEDNESDAY=

BOB RICHARDSON=

In 1955, dismantling operations had progressed almost to Shawano tank, and within a few days the highest rail crossing of the Continental Divide would be left to history and the elements. But for one last brief moment, the impressive three levels of trackage could be seen as they once were. *ABOVE:* Sighting from Shawano tank, seen at the left center of the photo, the snowshed could be faintly seen directly above the tank. The two points were, incredibly enough, separated by 2000 feet of altitude and four miles of track, some of which may be seen in the foregound. *LEFT:* In true mountain goat fashion, John Krause scurried down from his vantage point above Shawano tank to get a close-up of the scrap train pulling up to the tank. Tracking the narrow gauge required a sturdy and usually vintage auto, plus plenty of stamina for hiking and climbing to the mostly inaccessible locations near the tracks.

RIGHT: On a happier day in May of 1949, three 2-8-2s, 497, 490 and 498 blast east out of Sargent with 16 cars of coal and two refrigerator cars, trailed by a freshly painted caboose. The presence of the reefers is somewhat inexplicable as traffic out of the Gunnison area consisted almost exclusively of coal, some ore, fluorspar, cattle in season and some lumber. A likely explanation is that they are being hauled from the soon-to-be isolated Ouray line to Alamosa. In any event, the grade is 1.88%, the engines are making a run for the approaching 4%, spring is in the air, and the sound is stirring. *BELOW:* Sargent's *raison d'être* was as a helper station for the western slope of Marshall Pass, and it was at one time even an engine change point. It did boast a water tank, coaling facilities and yard facilities for setting out tonnage when doubling or tripling the hill. In 1955, the last of many C-16s, No. 268, paid a visit to Sargent and posed by the water tank. How many times in years gone by had she and her sister engines stood at the same spot? *BELOW RIGHT:* On a happier occasion in 1948, the 494 leads a 9 car Rocky Mountain Railroad Club special past the still-active depot on what was to be the last excursion to the Gunnison country from Salida.

Robert F. Collins

John Krause

Robert W. Andrews

LEFT: At Doyle, the Tomichi valley is wide, beautiful, and 8062 feet above sea level, which precludes most agricultural activities save for the raising of sheep and cattle. It was this lack of a traffic base that doomed the line to an early abandonment when the Crested Butte mine closed. The diminutive 268 heads east near Doyle, bound for Sargent to rescue the 480 on the scrap train. In the background rise the snow capped peaks of the West Elk Range. BELOW: In 1952, the one-time narrow gauge mainline was overgrown with weeds, but there were still stock cars to be switched at Parlin tank. Nineteen fifty-two would be the next to last year for this sort of activity, but the traditions of railroading were still observed as the 483 moved into position. RIGHT: Under a pillar of black smoke, the last Rio Grande freight to operate out of Gunnison pulls up to the water tank at Parlin, where once the South Park's Alpine Tunnel line came face to face with the mortal competition. The South Park became a part of the Colorado & Southern in 1898 and a minor cave-in inside the tunnel in 1910 gave the C&S an excuse to drop the Alpine Tunnel line. Eighteen miles of the old South Park mainline from Parlin up to Quartz was operated by the Rio Grande until 1934 as their Pitkin Branch. Little but the water tank and a few crossties to be loaded aboard for use elsewhere remained to greet the 480 on that September morning; and soon even these remnants would pass from the Tomichi valley.

John Krause

John Krause

John Krause

Gunnison

LEFT: Only a few train watchers and some railroad personnel were on hand in 1954 as 480 drifted into town with a caboose hop from Salida. Though the Gunnison station was still trim, little activity can be discerned and less is to come as the last year of operation approaches.
BELOW: Six years earlier, the scene was different as the 361 prepared to take a Rocky Mountain Railroad Club excursion west to Cimarron. The Little Mudhens came to the Gunnison area in 1916, and were regularly used through the Black Cañon and over Cerro Summit. The 361 was to power yet two more such trips before the June, 1949 abandonment; but this morning she is basking in the admiration of both the fans and the local citizens.

Robert W. Andrews   John Krause

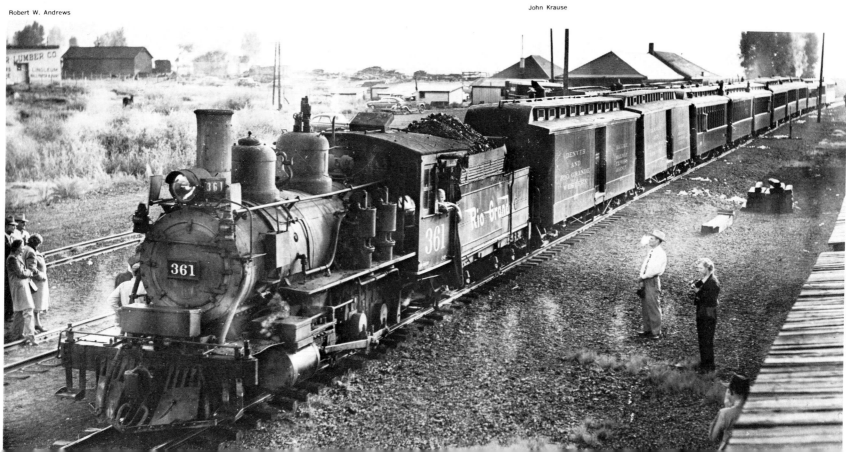

The yards and engine terminal at Gunnison were host to countless locomotives and cars during the 70 odd years of operation, but by the early 1950's, only one or two engines might be active. *ABOVE LEFT:* The 278 poses on the turntable. *ABOVE RIGHT:* The 268 sets out cars after returning to Gunnison from the clean up run to Sapinero. *LEFT:* The day's chores finished, the little Consolidation pauses at the tank for water.

Crested Butte Branch

Robert W. Andrews

By reason of serving the Colorado Fuel & Iron Company's coal mine, the Crested Butte Branch was responsible for 54% of the traffic that sustained the Marshall Pass line during its latter years. It was the only branch out of Gunnison capable of supporting the heaviest engines; K-37's and later K-36's were used as standard power up to 1948, providing daily service. *LEFT:* On September 18, 1948, the Rocky Mountain Railroad Club operated what was to be the last passenger train on the line. The 494 did the honors and in this scene is shown crossing the Taylor River at Almont.

Just before the mines closed in 1952, John Krause photographed the 480 and 483 at work on the branch. *ABOVE RIGHT:* The 480 switching the almost-deserted yard at Crested Butte as the West Elk mountains stand sentinel. *BELOW RIGHT:* The 483 pauses for water in front of the geological formation for which the area is named. *FAR RIGHT:* The train switched out, the 483 heads for Gunnison with a trainload of fine semi-anthracite. Interestingly, the Crested Butte area comprises the only deposit of anthracite coal west of the Mississippi and the only deposit outside of Pennsylvania that was commercially worth mining.

John Krause

John Krause John Krause

Philip R. Hastings

Philip A. Ronfor

Besides coal, seasonal stock movements were the only other source of traffic on the Crested Butte Branch. In September of 1952, photographers Phil Ronfor and Phil Hastings caught the 278 handling such a movement from Gunnison to Jack's Cabin for sheep loading. *ABOVE:* The end of the day found the 278 running in reverse back to Gunnison. But the day had begun early when the Consolidation pulled up to the tank at Jack's Cabin *(LEFT)*, pinned the caboose, and shoved the empty stock cars into the siding to begin the tedious loading process. As mentioned previously, the tank was moved to Jack's Cabin from the Villa Grove station on the Valley Line. *RIGHT:* The trainman on the roof brings the next empty to a stop in front of the loading chute as the woolies mingle about, blissfully unaware of their destination. The fall of 1952 proved to be the end, of both the fluted dome C-16 Consolidation and the stock business north of Gunnison.

Philip R. Hastings

The trim stone station of the South Park at Gunnison was constructed in 1882, shortly after the railroad finally arrived in town, having lost the race to the Rio Grande. It served that line and its successors, the Denver, Leadville and Gunnison, the Union Pacific, Denver and Gulf, and finally the Colorado and Southern until 1911, when the Rio Grande assumed jurisdiction over the recently isolated C&S operations in the Gunnison area. Whatever the faults of the South Park might have been, their stonework and construction techniques, which resembled closely those along the parent Union Pacific, were not one of them, for many of the structures have survived not only the railroad itself but also the ravages of time and the elements. Regrettably, the Gunnison station, which had served as a home for many years, was torn down in 1956 to make room for a highway. *LEFT:* In this 1955 scene, 268 chugs past the structure with a scrap train to begin dismantling the track that once was intended to become the Utah extension of the Denver, South Park and Pacific.

The Baldwin Branch

The Baldwin Branch was originally constructed to be the Denver Leadville and Gunnison's Utah extension, but the Rio Grande won the race and it ended up being that ill-starred line's furthest westward extension. The coal traffic generated by its mines supported the Alpine Tunnel line for a number of years. After Alpine was abandoned in 1911 it was operated by the Rio Grande under lease from the Colorado & Southern and finally purchased in 1937. The semi-anthracite coal was popular for home heating in those days and traffic held up well until about 1950. Ironically, the abandonments of the Black Cañon and Valley lines were responsible for much of the traffic loss, as much of the coal mined on the branch had been sold in Montrose, Ouray, and Alamosa. *ABOVE AND RIGHT:* On Memorial Day weekend in 1948, the line was still active and the 268 in pre-1949 basic black, rolled back to Gunnison with six cars of Castleton coal. Light bridges which precluded the use of power heavier than the C-16's ensured the survival of the last two examples of the once-numerous mountain mules into the 1950s. The coal, cattle, alpine meadows and snow-capped mountains all typified the branch in its later days.

Robert W. Andrews

Robert W. Andrews

40

The Sapinero Line

During most of the 1930's and 1940's, the ex-Crystal River Little Mudhens, Nos. 360 and 361, were regular power on the Black Cañon line and later on the Sapinero line, but by 1951 the C-21's had been scrapped and 278 was being utilized as sole power on the occasions when it was necessary to serve the branches. *LEFT:* On Sept. 20, 1952, the 70 year old 2-8-0 polished the rails of the former narrow gauge mainline, hauling boxcars to the mill at Sapinero for flourspar loading, and returning *(RIGHT)* with an impressive string of loaded stock cars. Though 278 had but a few more trips to make in her active career, she rounded out seventy years of service in a grand manner.

Philip A. Ronfor

It was left to sister 2-8-0 No. 268, veteran of the 1949 Chicago Railroad Fair and star of the movie *Denver and Rio Grande*, to perform the final rites at Sapinero on September 28, 1954. With her Grande Gold and black livery looking a little the worse for wear, the last of the once numerous narrow-gauge 2-8-0's ran from Gunnison to Sapinero to clean out the remaining freight cars before the scrappers showed up. A number of photographers were on hand to record the last trip, including a visiting trainman from the Susquehanna Railroad in New Jersey. John Treen had gone to Gunnison first to get a few pictures on what had become an annual vacationtime pilgrimage to Colorado, and in talking to some of the brothers at Gunnison, he found out about the last run to Sapinero that day. *ABOVE LEFT:* Arriving at Sapinero just ahead of the train, he recorded this overview of the town. It was a fortunate occurence, for the later construction of the Blue Mesa Dam would inundate this entire area almost to the western limits of Gunnison. *ABOVE:* There had not been a train in Sapinero in over a year, and the teacher at the little one room schoolhouse was wise enough to realize that the clean-up train would very likely be the last; declaring an impromptu recess, she brought the children out to the fence to watch the train. *LEFT:* Arriving in town with only an outfit car for a caboose, the 268 turned on the wye before grabbing hold of the

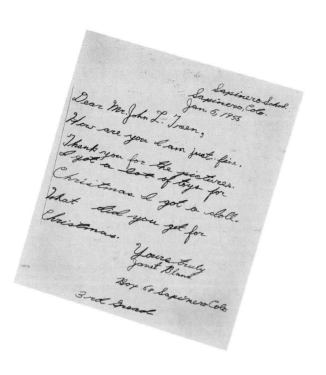

Sapinero School
Sapinero, Colo.
Jan. 5, 1955

Dear Mr. John L. Treen;

How are you I am just fine.
Thank you for the pictures.
I got a lot of toys for
Christmas I got a doll.
What did you get for
Christmas.

Yours truly
Janet Bland

Box 60 Sapinero Colo

3rd Grad

cars for the return trip. *ABOVE RIGHT:* Their train made up, the crew prepares to depart under the thoughtful gazes of both the town's old folks and the children. The back of the school is just visible past the front of the 268. *BELOW RIGHT:* The little Consolidation spreads a cloud of coal smoke over the town of Sapinero for the last time. As the bark of the exhaust fades away, the little town is left with only silence and its memories. There was to be a poignant postscript to the story, however; for photographer Treen had been so taken by the children and their interest in the little train that he took down all of their names. Upon returning home to New Jersey, he made up a little packet of photos taken that day and mailed one to each of the children. Shortly thereafter, there came back in the mail a letter from each of the little ones, proclaiming in awkward scrawl their thanks for the thoughtfulness of a visitor from far away who gave each of them a memento of that special day.

The Black Cañon

LEFT: The scene at Sapinero was a little happier in 1948 as the 361 brought one of the several excursions to operate through the Black Cañon by the Sapinero schoolhouse. With freshly laundered white flags and green coaches, the train will pause briefly before proceeding into the granite depths of the canyon. *RIGHT:* In recent decades, the presence of television camera crews on excursions have been a common sight; but in 1949, the presence of Movietone News cameraman Jean DuBois on the last run to Cimarron was a truly notable occurence. In this scene, the photographer cranks off a few stills as his Bolex stands in the foreground and the conductor observes the action. *BELOW:* Following a photo stop at the Curecanti Needle, the 361 drifts along the Gunnison River towards Cimarron as the passengers crowd every conceivable vantage point for a view of the 1,000 foot rock walls and roaring river that had captivated tourists in days of yore. Today the 361, the railroad, and even the scenery itself have passed into limbo, for Curecanti is the location of the dam which has flooded not only the canyon but much of the country east to Gunnison. *BELOW RIGHT:* On an appropriately grey afternoon, the 361 dusts the canyon walls with coal smoke as she heads the last passenger train back to Gunnison. One day later, the line will be officially abandoned and sister engine 360 will begin the somber duty of tearing up the line. The trestle will be left, however, to provide a county road through the Black Cañon for fishermen and others seeking to view the beauties once so eloquently trumpeted by the railroad. Thoughtful gesture though it was, the road could never duplicate the echoes of exhaust and chime whistles or the squeal of car flanges that this Bob Collins photo preserves.

Ross Grenard

Robert F. Collins

Robert W. Andrews

LEFT: At Crystal Creek, the railroad bade farewell to the river, and climbed up one of the side canyons to Cimarron. On May 30, 1949, the last of a long line of narrow-gauge passenger trains paused for a portrait on the trestle amidst the elements that made the Black Cañon what it was. Today, only the trestle remains to show man's influence and the 278 has been enshrined upon it by the National Park Service. On September 13, 1882, the first Rio Grande passenger train reached Cimarron; the last departed on May 30, 1949. During those years the water tank and the cottonwoods that overhung them witnessed a parade of narrow gauge activity unparalled in history, for its location between the canyons to the east and Cerro Summit to the west made the little community an important point on the Third Division; first as a helper station and meal stop in mainline days and later as a subdivision point where Gunnison and Montrose crews traded trains before returning to their respective terminals. The latter operation was mandated by the inability of the Mudhens to operate over the light trestles in the Black Cañon coupled with the necessity to utilize their greater tractive effort on the 4% grade to Cerro Summit. *RIGHT:* Since the track west of there had been condemned for passenger service, the postwar excursions all terminated at Cimarron where the trains were wyed and the engines serviced in a setting of placid beauty that belied the impending doom of the line. On the September 1948 Rocky Mountain Railroad Club excursion, the length of the wye and the fact that Cerro Summit literally begins at the west wye switch necessitated two passes to get the train turned. On the last run, the signs of abandonment were already visible as 361 drank for the last time beneath the trees that had grown to maturity with the railroad and would see its passing within the next few weeks.

Ross Grenard

Robert W. Andrews

Robert W. Andrews

Cerro Summit

Cerro Summit was not a picturesque mountain crossing in the sense of Cumbres, Marshall, or Lizard Head; but rather was simply 12.3 miles of uniform 4% grade between Cimmaron on the east and Cedar Creek on the west. The climb through the Squaw Hills was necessitated by the impossibility of constructing a railroad line through the lower reaches of the Black Cañon. Originally intended as a temporary expedient, Cerro Summit became a permanent member of the Rio Grande's 4% Club when all the surveys indicated that it was the only feasible route available to the builders. *ABOVE:* The two last runs over Cerro Summit occurred on May 27th and 28th in 1949; the 361 is seen climbing the grade against a prophetically darkening sky, hauling the last cars of Crested Butte coal west to Montrose. *LEFT:* The train approaches the summit passing track; the Y shaped sign at left warned the flanger operator in the wintertime to lift the flanger blades from between the rails to clear the switches ahead. *ABOVE RIGHT:* Three loads and a caboose was maximum tonnage for the 361, so three trips to the summit were necessary in order to get the whole train over the hill. In this view, the 361 has pulled up to the summit on the main, cut off the train and turned on the wye track to the right. The outside frame 2-8-0 is now backing down to couple up to the train again; the three loads of coal will be shoved into the passing track at the left and the 361 and the hack will drop back down to Cimmaron again to grab three more gons and repeat the procedure. *BELOW RIGHT:* On May 28th, Mudhen No. 456 hauled a train of empties east from the soon-to-be-isolated Montrose-Ouray segment and is seen here just east of Montrose. Since the K-27's tonnage rating was 308 tons from Montrose to Cedar Creek, and only 183 tons up the west slope of the grade, we can safely assume that two and perhaps three trips up the hill were necessary before freight service officially ended and the first break in the Circle became fact.

Montrose

Ross Grenard

Robert F. Collins

Montrose was the first community of any size reached by the narrow gauge after leaving Gunnison, and after 1906 became one of the select group of three rail junctions on the railroad. Relatively light tonnage, grades averaging less than 1%, and light rail kept more modern power off the 75 mile line to Grand Junction and ensured operation up to the end of steam of George Gould era 4-6-0's such as the 784 *(seen at LEFT),* which handled the overnight Denver-Montrose *Mountaineer* and assorted 2-8-0's and Mikes which served the freight needs of the area, and of the North Fork Branch to Somerset. The engine terminal at Montrose consisted of service facilities plus a two stall roundhouse, which made up in photo opportunities what it lacked in quantity of power assigned. *BELOW:* An 1881 Baldwin 2-8-0, the 340, poses for her portrait at Montrose in 1949. *RIGHT:* Two years later finds K-27 No. 454 occupying the same spot; in the background, looking almost as large as the locomotive, is a standard gauge drop bottom gon, apparently spotted for cinder loading.

After June of 1949, the narrow-gauge lines out of Montrose were transferred to the jurisdiction of the Grand Junction Division and operations were limited to runs to Ridgway and Ouray. Right up until the abandonment of the Rio Grande Southern, Mudhens were kept at Montrose to handle livestock movements off the RGS. *LEFT*: In the fall of 1946, Bob Collins caught the 456 leaving Montrose with a sizeable train of empty stock cars bound for Ridgway, most likely intended for sheep loading at Placerville or Lizard Head on the RGS. Note the unusual double derail at the left, protecting both the narrow and standard gauged rails.

The end of the RGS also meant the end of the "Mudhens" out of Montrose. The 318, an ex-Florence & Cripple Creek 2-8-0, was the last operable narrow gauge locomotive at Montrose, and during the last years handled switching (using idler cars) and such trips to Ouray as were required. The last run to Ouray was made in March of 1953. *BELOW*: In the summer of 1952, John Krause caught the 1896 Baldwin Consolidation heading south on its occasions through the sage brush covered hills of the Uncompahgre Valley in a scene that might have been taken years before.

John Krause

Robert F. Collins

Ridgway

Ridgway, named for the D&RG's Chief Engineer who constructed the Rio Grande Southern, once billed itself as the "Home of the Galloping Goose". It was here that most RGS shopwork was performed after the bankrupt company ceased farming out the work to the Grande at Alamosa. *BELOW:* On October 3, 1946, Goose No. 4 awaited passengers in front of the joint station that had witnessed so much narrow gauge activity, while the agent's 1941 Ford was parked prudently under the eaves.

Robert F. Collins

Robert F. Collins

The last major shopwork at Ridgway occurred in the spring of 1950 when the Geese were converted into their tourist hauling configuration. *BELOW:* Nos. 3 and 4 receive their various modifications, while a visiting railfan looks on, in an era innocent of the FRA and OSHA. *LEFT:* At the same time, the crew found time to perform some repairs to No. 20, remove her greasepaint and restore the front number plate after her *Ticket to Tomahawk* movie role. Despite almost total austerity, the old girl did get a green boiler, proper striping, and white driver tires, but the clipper ship that decorated the tender was left intact, and provided a conversation piece until the post-abandonment restoration of No. 20 by the Rocky Mountain Railroad Club.

Robert F. Collins

The area around the RGS shops at Ridgway contained a collection of both active and inactive narrow gauge equipment of all sorts and conditions in a bittersweet setting that indicated both the decline in fortunes of the road and the vitality that still existed. *LEFT:* In 1949, the original Galloping Goose, No. 2, slumbered through an August afternoon in company with the crippled rotary and wedge plow 02. *BELOW LEFT:* Two years later, the RGS' last acquired locomotive, ex-Rio Grande Mikado No. 461, and leased Mike No. 452 posed on the roundhouse lead next to 2-8-0 No. 74, which would soon lead the last steam passenger train over the line. *BELOW RIGHT:* A closer look at the disabled rotary. Shooting the right side, Sam Fredericks spared us the vision of the gaping wound in the left side caused by the boiler explosion that put the rotary out of service.

Ross Grenard

Ross Grenard   Sam Fredericks

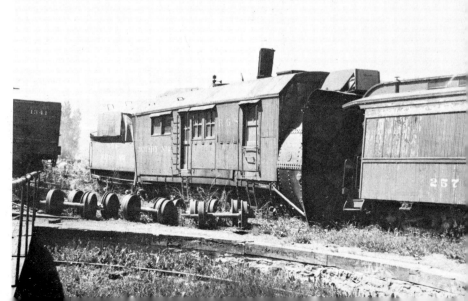

If the shop area at Ridgway offered much of interest to the trainwatcher, the departure yard and Rio Grande interchange north of the station provided little to indicate a traffic volume sufficient to support the railroad. *ABOVE:* On May 23, 1950, only a lone outfit car was on hand as the 455 prepared to leave with 12 empty boxcars for concentrate loading. Number 74, an 1898 Brooks 2-8-0, was the next to last power acquired by the RGS and had two notable distinctions. First, it had served three legendary narrow gauge lines previously: the Colorado & Northwestern, the Denver Boulder & Western, and the Colorado & Southern. Secondly, its original Stephenson valve gear had been replaced by Walschaerts motion in 1926, which required the addition of the curiously canted cylinders so apparent in photos of the engine. Purchased in March of 1949, its first starring role was to be the Memorial Day weekend excursion of the Rocky Mountain Railroad Club. Unfortunately, steaming problems developed soon after leaving Ridgway and the excursion ground to a halt amid the blooms of spring wildflowers. *RIGHT:* While passengers gathered around the engine with expressions of apprehension, puzzlement, and disbelief, the late Morris Abbot (seen in the left foreground) stoically recorded the situation with his Rollei while two future presidents of the club engaged in consultation with the Master Mechanic over what course of action to take. Perhaps the enforced idleness of the 74 had something to do with her problems, for she had sat in the yard of a Denver equipment dealer for four years gathering rust before the RGS purchased her.

Robert F. Collins

Ross Grenard

RIGHT: Regular passenger service still operated over the RGS in 1949, and at Valley View siding, the 74 and its first excursion held the main while Goose No. 5 rolled by on the passing track bound for Ridgway with the U.S. Mail, express, and some non-railfan passengers. The newly-repainted office car B-20 decorated the rear of the train and future chronicler of the narrow gauge, Bob LeMassena, decorated the rear platform, perched above the RMRRC's hand-painted tailsign, while noted historian, Ed Haley, on the ground, observed the operation. A few weeks before the excursion, a volunteer group from the Club had given Otto Mears' erstwhile private car a coat of Pullman Green paint, and even on that cloudy morning it lent a note of class to the occasion.

Ross Grenard

Robert W. Andrews

John Krause

The summit of Dallas Divide is dominated by the Uncompaghre Mountains to the south, and they provided an impressive background for countless photos of Ridgway bound trains over the years. They were particularly impressive in the spring and their beauty is enduring, as can be seen in these two views separated by five years of time. *ABOVE LEFT:* Goose No. 5 crosses the highway in May of 1949, running in regular service. *LEFT:* Five years earlier, the immortal Otto Perry caught leased Rio Grande Mike 454 preparing to descend the 4% grade. The 454's train is of note, for it was photographed on June 19, 1944, and its consist no doubt includes a few cars of yellow cake which was refined into U-235 for use in the Manhattan Project. It seems incongruous that the 1904 Baldwin and the archbar-trucked cars are a vital part of a weapons system that included the most brilliant physicists of the day, the most advanced technology available, and a B-29 bomber named *Enola Gay*, all of which would combine to bring to an end the most destructive war in history. *ABOVE:* In August of 1952, the bright sky belied the somber occasion as the 461 headed south near Dallas Divide with a collection of outfit cars, the 455's tender, and caboose 0400, bound for Rico. The Southern was officially dead, and the odd consist was the first of many scrap trains to operate that fall, as the last and saddest chapter of the Southern's long history commenced to unfold. *ABOVE RIGHT:* On May 21, 1949, the Dolores bound Goose met the 455 and a freight returning from Telluride on the south slope of Dallas Divide at Wades. The siding at Wades was stub-ended at the south, and Goose No. 5 pulled in the north switch, let the extra pass, and then backed out on to the main again, resulting in the rather unusual scene depicted. Since the 3% grade out of the San Miguel River valley was a bit taxing, the Goose took the siding to allow the freight to maintain its stride. *BELOW RIGHT:* Brown's Tank was the first water stop on the RGS, some 22 miles out of Ridgway; here an immaculately conditioned No. 20 was caught by Phil Ronfor's Graflex on May 30, 1947.

Otto Perry, Collection of Ross Grenard

Philip A. Ronfor

Placerville

Robert F. Collins

Placerville was the first community of any size encountered by the RGS south of Ridgway and its frame station was the only open agency between Ridgway and Telluride during the last few decades. It was a major shipping point for sheep: in the spring, the woolies were brought to the high pastures to graze; in the fall, the railroad hauled them out again to the packing houses of Denver, Omaha, and Kansas City. *ABOVE:* In the fall of 1946, Bob Collins caught Goose No. 4, running as Train 376, pausing at the Placerville station to take aboard some cans of cream and a few sacks of mail bound for points north.

RIGHT: On September 1, 1951, No. 74 drifts past the depot on its way to Telluride with the last passenger train. The grades of Dallas Divide are behind the Brooks 2-8-0, but soon it will start working steam up the San Miguel River Valley. *BELOW:* As the swollen waters of the San Miguel flow heedlessly by, the crew of Extra 455 East prepares to do some switching at Placerville in the spring of 1948. The freight has come through from Telluride and will probably add a few cars to its consist before tackling the 3% grade of Dallas Divide. Obtained by the RGS in an equipment trade with the Rio Grande, the 455 was long a stalwart performer out of Ridgway. Its somewhat different appearance when compared with other K-27's was the result of a 1944 rebuilding after a runaway on the 4% grade near Valley View. The cab and tender from a 600 series Rio Grande 2-8-0 were used in the rebuild and altered its profile considerably.

Ross Grenard

Robert W. Andrews

Vance Junction and the Telluride Branch

Vance Junction, where the Telluride Branch diverged from the main line, probably saw more traffic than any point between Durango and Ridgway, but for most of its years consisted of a closed station, a windowless and truckless coach used for storage, a coal pocket, and a small yard. In the days after passenger service into Telluride ceased; mail, express, passengers, and L.C.L. were transferred to an RGS truck at Bilk Siding, 1.4 miles north, where the railroad and highway were within closer proximity, leaving Vance even more lonely than ever. *ABOVE LEFT:* In this 1946 Bob Collins shot, Goose No. 4 is northbound, passing the Junction switch. *ABOVE RIGHT:* A little less than four years later, the same Goose, rebuilt into a tourist hauler posed on the trestle spanning the south fork of the San Miguel, on the occasion of its first charter trip from Ridgway. Again, Bob Collins was present to record a classic view of the wierd and wonderful machine which saved the RGS, and Mears Peak named in honor of its builder. *RIGHT:* On May 28, 1949, No. 74, having overcome earlier steaming problems, raises her pops triumphantly at the 9007 foot elevation of Pandora Basin, where the Telluride Branch came to a dead end in the shadow of Mt. Ajax. The Narrow Gauge Boomer stands next to the Smuggler-Union Mill, which processed gold and silver ore from the Tomboy, Black Bear, and Sheridan mines, as well as its namesake. In the background, carved out of the mountain, can be seen the road to the mines in Ingraham Basin, and the tailing from the mill. Although the flush times when the Rothschild Brothers purchased the Tomboy for $2,000,000 have long passed, the ore cars spotted at the mill indicate that the mining industry which provided the *raison d'etre* for the RGS still provided its principal source of traffic.

Ross Grenard

Ross Grenard

ABOVE: Two years and a few months later, the 74 drew the last passenger train to Telluride and posed again before the mountain backdrop. By this time, the mines had switched to trucks and the end was near, not only for the railroad, but for the great days of the town itself where once 21 saloons, countless pleasure palaces and an opera house had catered to the tastes of the populace. But for one last Saturday night, the 132 passengers on the historic trip would bring back the glory days of the Circle to the streets and to the bar and dining room of the Sheridan Hotel. *RIGHT:* "All Aboard for Ophir" . . . on the May 1949 excursion, the train dropped down the branch, turned the 74 at Illium, and backed down a mile to Vance Junction and onto the main for the run to Lizard Head. Here the conductor passes a highball as the last stragglers jump aboard the gondola cars that were standard passenger equipment on these jaunts.

Ophir

The Ophir Loop was to the Rio Grande Southern what Horseshoe Curve was to the Pennsylvania or the spiral tunnels to the Canadian Pacific: the crowning glory of its engineering technology and the professional response to a seemingly impassable bit of topography. In the case of Ophir, the seven trestles and the 24 degree curves were mandated by an inability to follow the San Miguel from Butterfly to Matterhorn, while maintaining any sort of viable gradient. To overcome this, two levels of track were carved out of the side of Yellow Mountain, with the high line alternating between rock cuts and trestles to provide a spectacle almost beyond belief. *RIGHT:* Even in death it was almost unbelievable, as John Krause caught the 461 and its scrap train crossing Howard Fork of the San Miguel and preparing to double back upon itself, as Vermillion Peak looks down upon Ophir, the railroad, and the workings of the Silver Bell Mine. The last tourists have gone, and the boxcars no longer wait to be loaded, but for one last moment the glory lives on.

John Krause

John Krause

Ross Grenard

On earlier and happier occasions, the 74 had performed on the Howard Fork trestle for the fans. *LEFT:* The 2-8-0 holds the undivided attention of a photo line in 1949, while the still snow-covered flanks of Sunshine Peak look down. The gash in the mountain carrying the high line of the track is just visible where the engine smoke is beginning to dissipate. *ABOVE:* In 1951, she arrives at Ophir with what would be the last steam passenger train on the RGS, canting to the 17 degree curvature of the trestle's end.

The RGS station at Ophir also served as the Post Office for the community, and in addition to being one of the most photographed depots in the country, also achieved a degree of immortality through being produced as an HO scale structure in kit form. Named for the Biblical location of King Solomon's Mines, Ophir's mines lived up to their namesake and produced fabulous amounts of precious metals over the years. The Alta Mine even had an aerial tramway whose bucket conveyor fed ore directly to boxcars spotted under the head house just behind the station. *BELOW:* In 1952, the 461 paused briefly at Ophir from her duties on the scrap train. A number of the red spruce trestles in the Ophir area were left intact after the dismantling and are reported to be as sound today as the day they were set in place. We may wonder if any of the marvels of our 1970's technology will enjoy equal longevity.

John Krause

LEFT: In August of 1952, John Krause arrived in Colorado just in time to record the final rites of the RGS; here the 461 heads south out of Ophir, bound for Lizard Head. The scrapper has dropped off his cars at Ophir and is heading out to size up the job that lays ahead. After the reconnaissance, he will return to Ophir to pick up the cars and begin pulling up the rails. The brooding and awesome mountain and the gathering stormclouds almost suggest that Nature is offended by the removal of the slim gauge rails from her environs.

RIGHT: At Matterhorn, 1.7 miles from Ophir station, the RGS came back to relatively solid ground. It was here in May of 1949 that the 74 cut off from its excursion train to rescue Goose No. 4, running as Train 376, and shove it into the siding. The Geese were not without their mechanical problems and incidents of this nature occurred from time to time. *BELOW:* Returning from Dolores on the 1947 Memorial Day excursion, leased Rio Grande 2-8-0 No. 319, an ex-Florence & Cripple Creek hog, pauses for water at Trout Lake Tank as the passengers inspect the train and view the lofty San Miguel's and the man made lake whose waters generated kilowatts for the Western Colorado Power Company. The weathered sign board and water tank typified the state of lineside facilities during the final years.

Ross Grenard

Philip A. Ronfor

Lizard Head

Lizard Head was the highest point on the Rio Grande Southern, the summit of the San Miguels, and registered the highest snowfalls of any point on the line, some 400 inches on occasion. Windswept and cold throughout the years, it was also a place where one could point a camera in any direction and obtain good pictures. In May of 1949, the Rocky Mountain Railroad Club excursion emerged from the snowsheds *(LEFT)* and posed for photographs *(RIGHT)* against the background of the snowy San Miguels while the train crew checked things over and set up retainers prior to turning the train and backing down the line for a photo stop.

Robert F. Collins

Lizard Head Peak was the most prominent geological feature of the pass, thrusting its head up some 13,106 feet above sea level. During the season of steam excursions on the RGS, it was a standard photo stop, and here are two perspectives of the view immortalized by William Henry Jackson in 1890: LEFT: No. 20 on its southbound trip from Ridgway to Dolores in May of 1947; *BELOW:* No. 74 in 1949, with considerably more snow in the foreground, still left from the incredible winter which lingered even into June. RIGHT: Another and less famous perspective of Lizard Head was caught by Phil Ronfor as the scrap train dropped down the 3% grade towards Coke Ovens and Rico. In the foreground can be seen the lower Gallagher Trestle *(FAR RIGHT)* and the nature of the descent can be observed by comparing the two track levels.

Philip A. Ronfor

Philip A. Ronfor

73

Rico

Rico came into prominence in 1879, when a major silver strike occurred in the area, and remained a major producer of lead carbonates and silver for many years. Tapping its traffic was one of the goals of Otto Mears in constructing the RGS, and the loss of the mine business was a major factor in precipitating the 1951 abandonment. It was also the division point and in later years most Ridgway freights originated and terminated there. *LEFT:* In 1946, Bob Collins caught the Ridgway bound Goose at the Rico station awaiting departure, as two lady fans engaged in some picture-taking at the freight house. For the Geese, Rico was more of an intermediate stop as they began their runs at Dolores. *BELOW:* On May 30, 1947, No. 20 made a brave show of arriving in the rain with the Rocky Mountain Railroad Club excursion, as so many specials had during the pre-Silver Crash days. The leaking flues which were to preclude her use on the next day were becoming apparent, but she carried on the 36 miles to Dolores, which fortunately was mostly downgrade.

Philip A. Ronfor

Robert F. Collins

Dolores

Dolores, at a 6,550 foot elevation, was the low point on the RGS and trains in both direction had to climb out of town. It was also a major shipping point for agricultural products, chiefly beans and lumber. Most of this business moved via Durango, and in most instances freights out of Durango tied up here. At one time, the McPhee Lumber narrow gauge connected with the RGS here, making it the only junction of the RGS with a non-Rio Grande Line. On May 31, 1947, Phil Ronfor arose early to photograph the activity at Dolores, which included *(RIGHT)* Goose No. 4 ready to depart for Ridgway, and *(ABOVE)* a collection of motive power including Goose No. 7, Rio Grande Mudhen 452, the incapacitated 20, and ex-F&CC 2-8-0 No. 319, which would pinch hit for the ten-wheeler on the return trip. Though the weather was less than optimum for photography, particularly with the low ASA ratings of film at that time, the scent of coal smoke was in the air and Mr. Ronfor's artistic talents were put to good use in recording the atmosphere which prevailed that morning.

Philip A. Ronfor

Philip A. Ronfor

The last and saddest railroad activity at Dolores occurred in September of 1952, when 42 was fired up to handle dismantling chores on the south end. *LEFT:* Shown here at what remained of the Dolores engine terminal, it was to work from north of Dolores and eventually ended up snowed in near Mancosa in November. When the decision was made in the spring of 1953 to use Geese to handle the remaining dismantling, the nineteenth-century Baldwin 2-8-0 had the dubious distinction of being the last RGS engine in steam as she ran from Grady Siding to Durango. Built for the Rio Grande in 1887, and originally numbered 420, it was sold to the RGS in 1916. In later years she was mainly used as a helper during stock season or for snow bucking since it was relatively light and could be rerailed more easily. Originally scheduled to be scrapped, 42 was purchased for the former Narrow Gauge Museum at Alamosa, and has since operated at the now defunct Magic Mountain theme park near Golden. Prior to 1948, the Rio Grande Southern connected at Dolores with the Montezuma Lumber Company's railroad, successor to the old McPhee operations, which brought in many a car of freshly milled boards. From 1941 to 1946, power was provided by ex-Rio Grande 271, once the Durango switcher (see page 82). In 1946, Bob Collins caught the kit-bashed 2-8-0 just before a scorched crown sheet ended the Baldwin's career.

Sam Fredericks

Durango-Dolores passenger service was discontinued in 1942, so photos of Geese in regular service on that stretch of the line are rather rare. In this photo of No. 4 at Hesperus in 1939, can be seen some of the reasons for the early demise. No passengers and very little mail or express appear in sight, and the depot itself will be burned to the ground in an accidental fire a few years later.

Robert F. Collins

Robert F. Collins

Robert F. Collins

LEFT: On October 2, 1946, the *Lucius Beebe Special* began its pilgrimage out of Durango and was recorded just clearing the town. Travelling the full length of the RGS to Ridgway, Ten-wheeler No. 20 appropriately did the honors over the first portion of the run. *ABOVE:* Although "October's Bright Blue Weather" was not in evidence, the veteran of the Golden Circle stormed along most impressively near Porters, with freshly-laundered white flags indicating that this was not a normal freight movement. *RIGHT:* A few miles further on, the omnipresent Bob Collins snapped a rear view of the special and recorded for posterity Alfred E. Perlman (at the left) and Charles Clegg enjoying the scenery. Mr. Perlman is the host aboard the office cars B-2 and B-7 in his official capacity as Chief Engineer of the Rio Grande, making a periodic inspection of the property. Since in the years to come, the two individuals' association with the narrow gauge will be of such a different nature, one might well wonder what their thoughts were at the moment.

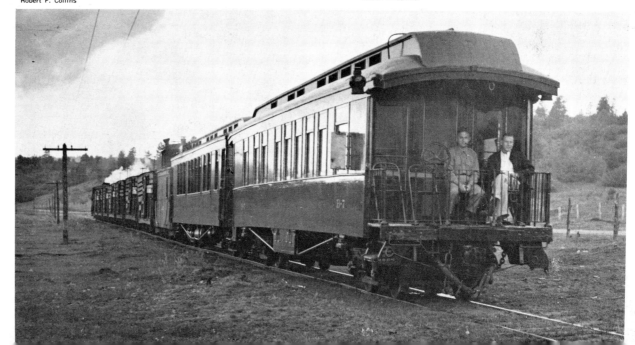

LEFT: With white flags snapping in the sunlight of a June morning in 1950, the 464 brings a Rico bound freight across the curved trestle at Franklin Junction. Spring has come to the La Plata's, and with it the hope that the railroad will survive another year. The trestle over Lightner Creek was a popular photo location and figured in several of the RGS' disasters at various times. The 464 had been shopped the previous year and would serve both the RGS and the Rio Grande until it was moved to California for display at Knott's Berry Farm.

John Krause

John Krause   Ross Grenard

Durango

At Durango, the southern terminus of the RGS, it was often difficult to delineate the two carriers' operations, for the Grande handled switching and engine servicing, and regularly leased engines to the Southern. *ABOVE RIGHT:* Such was the occasion on September 25, 1949, when leased Mudhen No. 464 served as the road engine on a stock train while RGS 74 lead the way as a helper for the 2.8% grade which lay ahead.

During the summers of 1950 and 1951, the Geese were regular visitors to Durango, albeit as tourist haulers. Unfortunately, trips out of Durango were not as numerous as those on the northern and more scenic portion of the line. Even so, it was a little bit like pre-1942 days to see Goose No. 5 *(BELOW RIGHT)* at the Durango station next to the roundhouse.

In *Mixed Train Daily*, Lucius Beebe first dubbed Durango "the narrow-gauge capital of the United States" and in the late 1940's and early 1950's this was expanded to include the whole world. The latter claim may not have been entirely justified, but the fact remains that the operations around Durango were most fascinating to observe in the days when lines converged from all points of the compass and were basically standard gauge operations somewhat miniaturized.

LEFT: Any yardmaster, operator, or master mechanic would be completely at home in this station scene as the switcher makes up a freight for Chama and the *Silverton's* equipment waits for the passengers to begin filing aboard. Since narrow gauge switch engines *per se* were never built, the versatile 2-8-0's performed these duties over the decades prior to 1951. *ABOVE:* In 1939, the 271 was assigned the task of switching Durango yard and is seen here going up to the west end of the yard to pick up a cut of cars. *BELOW:* In an era ignorant of jet travel, expressways, or other devisings of contemporary society; the 484 prepares for departure from the spacious Durango depot. As the fireman builds up steam pressure, the carman walks off to other tasks, and the Railway Express truck stands in the background. How much would we pay for a ticket now?

RIGHT: In June of 1950, an 1881-vintage C-19 class Consolidation was assigned as the Durango switcher, and the 345 was delighting tourists and fans alike with such movements as the evening wyeing of the *San Juan's* equipment. *BELOW RIGHT:* Two years later, the surviving Mudhens had taken over the yard assignment and the 453, bumped from the Silverton Branch by the 470's, ran out its final miles in what was to be the last regular job for the once ubiquitous K-27's. Later, the 464 would ring down the curtain on this class in the same yard assignment. *BELOW:* The Durango yard crew earned their money, but they were not so busy as to preclude a group picture, and here they are gathered around their locomotive in the traditional working garb of that era.

John Krause

John Krause

John Krause

John L. Treen

Ross Grenard

Philip R. Hastings

In December of 1953, the U.S. Army Transportation Corps, desiring to run an extended test on diesel locomotives for narrow gauge service, arranged to have their 4700N assigned to Durango for some two years. The locomotive was an Army design produced in

quantity by Whitcomb (which was at that time a sub-sidiary of the Baldwin Locomotive Works), but a number of the locomotives were also built by Davenport. In addition to 16 standard gauge units, Davenport also built two adjustable-gauge units: No. 4000 was adjustable from standard gauge up to 5'-6" gauge, while the 4700N went the other way from standard down to three foot. *FAR LEFT, ABOVE:* The little B-B unit developed a tractive effort about equal to that of a 2-8-0, so it was eventually decided to restrict the Little Monster to yard service, and she is seen here switching in front of the Durango depot in the summer of 1954. While dieselization was rumored for the Alamosa-Farmington line in 1956, a decline in carloadings vetoed any actual orders and 4700N and a larger General Electric six axle job which appeared in 1957 were the only non steam power to see service on the line until the purchase of an ex-Sumpter Valley diesel mechanical locomotive in 1963 to take over what remained of the switching chores.

The Durango enginehouse was located at the foot of Main Street and was a relatively informal terminal wherein few employees would bother the fan who sought to take pictures or merely walk through and savor the ambience of what was to become one of the U.S.'s last active steam roundhouses. *FAR LEFT, BELOW:* The freshly painted 492 has just received a full tender of coal and pulled up to spot a sister Mike under the dock. *LEFT:* The 480 slumbers in the Durango roundhouse in a timeless scene. A coal stove between each pit was needed to shed the raw chill of winter. *ABOVE RIGHT:* Durango engine terminal is a beehive of early morning activity; the 483 and 484 are lined up for a Chama freight and as the gang readies the engines under the watchful eyes of a pair of visiting fans, a fire hose slowly fills the 484's tank. The 476 on the adjacent track is lined up for the Silverton train, as evidenced by the phony oil headlight and diamond stack applied in deference to the *tourista*. *BELOW RIGHT:* In June of 1950, the 453 in the background stands dead, her fire pulled to allow some periodic repairs. By this time, the K-27 was active only in yard service. Pulling out on the table, it is not evident that the 464 will not be running on the Rio Grande today, but rather to Ridgway, for she is leased to the Rio Grande Southern in the next to last golden summer of RGS operation.

Robert F. Collins

John Krause

The Silverton Branch

John Krause

LEFT: In 1952, the Silverton Branch train was still very much a mixed, as attested by the 478 preparing to leave Durango on a sunny morning with eight empty boxcars for ore loading ahead of the caboose and coaches. In a familiar ritual of railroading, the blue flag protecting the workmen is removed as a machinist makes some last minute checks. Soon the traditional two short whistle blasts will sound and the 1923 Alco Mikado will lead its consist off for the Animas canyon. In the early years, when over 50 major mines produced ore concentrates as fast as the railroad could haul them away; at least two doubleheaded freights were dispatched from Durango daily and a regular switch job worked at Silverton. From the 1920's on, the mixed was generally able to handle such cars as were shipped save for an occasional movement of sheep to or from the high pastures. A combination of declining tonnage and assignment of the 2-8-2's, which tripled tonnage ratings, were basically responsible. *ABOVE:* In September of 1954, some extra passenger cars plus four cars of inbound freight resulted in 476 and 478 teaming up to attack the grade out of Hermosa with 15 cars. Their smoky glory and mingled exhausts recalled the days of C-16 Consolidations, 105-ton-per-engine ratings, and a world where national wealth was measured in terms of gold and silver. *RIGHT:* On an August morning in 1952, Mudhen No. 463 starts up the 2.5% grade out of Hermosa on the climb to Rockwood. As a general rule, the 470's were assigned to the summer operations, but today the ex-Vauclain compound is taking one of its last flings with a 10 car train.

John Krause

87

John Krause John Krause

Since the lower portion of the Animas Gorge was impossible to construct a railroad through, the Rio Grande engineering corps responded by building the High Line from Rockwood to Tacoma trestle to gain entrance to the only practical route to the riches of Silverton and the San Juans. Blasted out of the canyon face by workers lowered on ropes at an almost prohibitive (for 1882) cost of $100,000 per mile, it was and remains one of the greatest feats of American railroad engineering and made possible the construction of the rest of the railroad, although its strain on the limited resources of the company at the time was considerable. The one-and-a-quarter miles have evoked awe and admiration from almost four generations of passengers and doubtless was a major consideration in declaring the Silverton Branch a Civil Engineering Landmark. *LEFT:* In an August, 1952 scene, Mudhen No. 463 brings the Durango-bound mixed up the 1.42% grade from the river as the shadows begin to envelop the lower reaches of the gorge, and the afternoon sun highlights the nature of the topography against which the relatively primitive technology of the railroad's builders contended and prevailed. *FAR LEFT:* A year later, the 473 eases along the shelf at the prescribed 8 mph on its way to Silverton, and over the stone palisade constructed to ease the railroad's footing along the shelf. This water level view graphically illustrates the height of the track at this point and the nature of the lower gorge, which constituted the greatest natural barrier encountered by the Rio Grande between Denver and Silverton. *RIGHT:* After the High Line comes the descent down the 1.42% grade to Tacoma and the crossing of the Animas. In 1955, the 476 backs into position for a photo run with its freshly painted equipment. In contrast with 1954, two 470's did the honors on the excursion, although regrettably only one could be used at Tacoma because of the bridge loading.

Ross Grenard

The upper reaches of the Animas canyon offer spectacular vistas for both the train passenger and the photographer willing to make the effort to reach the exceptional photo locations available. *FAR LEFT:* Here in 1954, the train is dwarfed by the immensity of the mountains, the river, and the canyon walls as it heads north through an area where winter snowslides once blocked the line with great regularity, and which is entirely without population. *LEFT:* The 463 was a favorite of engine crews on the Silverton line, particularly for winter operations. It steamed well and was fitted with inside cylinder cocks especially for bucking snow. In August of 1952, John Krause caught the old girl smoking up the ecology of the Animas Canyon north of Elk Park, as Train 462 drifts down the river towards Durango; its capacity-load of tourists supplemented by eight loads of ore concentrates. Though the afternoon is gray, and the promise of a mountain storm hangs in the air, both the branch and the 463 will survive. Purchased in 1955 by Gene Autry for display at Melody Ranch, the survivor of 50 years of mountain railroading is currently being prepared for display at Antonito beside the Cumbres & Toltec Scenic Line. *BELOW:* In a rare appearance, U.S. Army 4700N assists the 476 on the Durango-Silverton leg of the annual Rocky Mountain Railroad Club's three day pilgrimage. The Little Monster's appearance that day caused some understandable wailing and gnashing of teeth, but in retrospect, the Davenport and the temporarily renumbered (for some eminently forgettable movie) K-27 did make an Odd Couple the likes of which hasn't been seen since. In this scene, they are on the last lap into Silverton and the one universal thought among the 350 passengers aboard is probably anticipation of a return down the canyon without benefit of the diesel age. *RIGHT:* On the first Sunday of September 1953, with only a caboose indicating that it operates as a mixed train, the 461 comes out of the canyon and into Baker Park for the final mile into Silverton as the peaks of the San Juans look down.

John Krause

John Krause

LEFT: In 1946, Bob Collins rode the mixed and this photo shows a little of what went on as the 453 switched stock cars for loading with sheep from the summer pastures above the timberline as the caboose and combine wait by the station. *RIGHT AND BELOW:* The veteran railroader returned to Silverton in the spring of 1950 and caught the 476 performing the switching chores in two scenes dominated by Grand Turk and Sultan Mountains. Though the date is May 18th, spring will not come to the 9300 foot altitudes for at least three weeks, and the hand of winter is still upon the land.

Robert F. Collins

Robert F. Collins

The Farmington Branch

Robert F. Collins

The Farmington Branch had one of the most unusual histories of all the narrow gauge branches. The 48-mile line came in fairly late compared to the other branches, being built in 1905. But the real anomaly of the branch was the fact that it was built to standard gauge, despite the fact that all the lines out of Durango were three foot gauge. Cars and locomotives were disassembled at Alamosa and shipped to Durango on the narrow gauge to furnish equipment to operate the line. The branch was apparently built because George Gould feared that the Santa Fe or more likely the Southern Pacific intended to build a standard gauge line to Durango to tap the coal traffic. He felt that building a standard gauge line would force the competition to interchange with the Rio Grande rather than attempt to build a parallel line, whereas the competitors could easily justify paralleling a narrow gauge line. Gould may have even intended to go all the way to Gallup in his continuing fued with Edward H. Harriman. By 1923, Harriman was gone and Gould, exhausted and depleted financially by his battles with Harriman in the west and the Pennsylvania Railroad in the east, had left the country for Europe where he had died in 1921; the year the branch was converted to narrow gauge. It struggled along for many years on what agricultural and lumber traffic it could generate, with once a week operations being the regular practice. As a rule, lighter power was assigned to the branch because the grade was only 1% northbound. LEFT: Although a Mudhen would be the usual power, on May 17, 1950 Bob Collins caught the 476, formerly of the *San Juan* pool, heading south from Durango with a consist of empty stock cars and general freight.

Within a year, major oil and gas discoveries in the Four Corners area would totally change the traffic patterns, cause an increase to almost daily service for the next decade, and insure the survival of the remaining narrow gauge into the 1960's. *RIGHT:* On the 1958 Rocky Mountain Railroad Club excursion, high water on the Silverton Branch caused a substitution of Farmington and the Aztec cliff dwellings for the Animas canyon. On the morning of May 31st, the 493 brought the train south near Bondad in a location which shows the semi-arid topography of the area and the La Plata's in the distance.

Robert F. Collins

95

Robert F. Collins

Robert F. Collins

LEFT: In 1960, the Illini Railroad Club went to Farmington behind the 480, seen here crossing the Animas at Bondad, still in Colorado. On this excursion, the gray skies were not a portent, for the line still had six years to go before the end came. *BELOW LEFT:* The 493 drifts south past the neat frame depot at Aztec, New Mexico and under the cottonwoods on its way to Farmington. A descending 1% grade down the Animas River made the first part of the trip a pleasure for the fireman, but the return more than made up for it with heavy trains of empty pipe cars, particularly after several hours switching at Farmington. During the early 1950's, Farmington and Aztec led all other stations on the Rio Grande in terms of dollar volume of business due to the tremendous volume of traffic generated by the oil and gas drillers. *BELOW:* There was plenty of switching to be done in Farmington, and in this scene, we see the old time brake club still being put to good use in tying down the handbrake on a gon. To the right are some of the cars of pipe responsible for the branch's prosperity. *RIGHT:* The switching completed, it's time for a drink before preparing to return to Durango.

Ron Ziel

Ron Ziel

Durango to Chama

Philip R. Hastings

John Krause

John Krause

Prior to 1951, the departure of Train 216, the *San Juan,* was an occasion of some import in Durango, for the train was a tangible link with the outside world in an era innocent of the jet plane and interstate highway. Just as departure times from Chicago and New York might be arranged for the convenience of the financial establishment, the 11:15 AM departure of the *San Juan* was arranged so as to allow the Durango banks to stow their Federal Reserve and other correspondent bank deposits aboard the RPO and express car. *LEFT:* In this 1949 scene, the carman stands by for an air test, and the head end mail and express is loaded, as a selection of vintage autos populate the station lot. *ABOVE:* On another occasion, the engineer of the *San Juan* and one of the roundhouse crew engage in small talk while awaiting the highball. The carmen's blue flag is still up, indicating it may be a while before the 483 is off to Chama, and the nature of the conversation is speculative: ranging from lodge affairs to politics, or from the future of the railroad to where the fish are biting. In a few moments the train will be on its way and another operational day will have reached full flower on the San Juan Extension.

ABOVE RIGHT: Heading east out of Durango, the *San Juan* has cleared Carbon Junction and is beginning the climb out of the Animas Valley to Falfa, one of two stretches of 2% grade between Durango and Chama. The 484 is obviously having little trouble with the grade, not suprisingly so in view of its four-car train, for the stack is clear and the safety valves are popping merrily. *RIGHT:* A few miles up the line, the 487 brings the 1954 Memorial Day excursion of the Rocky Mountain Railroad Club eastbound through the 20-degree curves near Falfa. The Chama-Durango line was constructed as cheaply as possible, and for this reason its most notable feature is a series of up and down, hill and dale curves and loops which were supposed to have been straightened out at a later date, but never were.

Philip R. Hastings

LEFT: After climbing to Falfa, the line drops downgrade into Florida, where Phil Hastings caught the alliterative Kiwanis Kolor Karavan on September 29, 1963, certainly an offbeat name for an excursion train. K-36 Mike No. 484 obviously has no intention of stopping for water as it moves the special east. *LOWER LEFT:* Ignacio, Colorado, was the site of the Southern Ute Agency, and because of various provisos in the tribe's treaty, the station there remained open almost up to the end of operations. Probably just as well that it did, for in the 1950's a nearby natural gas field resulted in extremely heavy freight business. In 1955, Michael Todd made use of the station in *Around the World in Eighty Days,* with Joe E. Brown cast as the operator. The depot was never repainted back to Rio Grande colors afterwards and it made a stunning sight in 1956 as a Rocky Mountain special rolled west behind the 490. *BELOW:* Not so fortunate was Allison, which was closed in the 1930's, but whose building remained intact almost until abandonment. In 1955, the Railroad Club special is seen passing the vacant building behind the 499.

Ross Grenard   John Krause

The 6013 foot elevation at Arboles made it the lowest point on the Alamosa-Durango line and it was the first piece of track to be ripped up, albeit replaced coincidentally by a new line when dam construction flooded the area in 1961. It also possessed another structural distinction in that its water tank was the salvaged tender of a standard gauge 1600 series 4-8-2 which had been scrapped in 1949. *ABOVE:* In September of 1956, the 488 and 482 brought a doubleheaded freight east on the now inundated track along the Rio San Juan. *RIGHT:* A few years earlier, 487 and 492 blast up the 1.27% grade east of Arboles along the Rio San Juan. Ahead lies a climb of 1850 feet to Chama, to be accomplished in a little over 40 miles, and the cresting of the Continental Divide at Azotea.

Every afternoon at 1:35, the east and westbound *San Juan's* met at Carracas, and only on exceptional occasions was either train late. On September 30, 1946, the 476 was in charge of the eastbound. After the end of passenger service, the comparatively short (39-car) Carracas siding was torn up and the name stricken from the operating timetable.

Six miles east of Carracas was the community of Pagosa Junction, or Gato, as the railroad referred to it after the abandonment of the Pagosa Springs Branch in the 1930's. Its feline name was derived from Gato (Cat) Creek, and it was a popular watering spot for both freight and passenger trains. *RIGHT:* A freight extra pauses in front of the log depot which had previously served at Amargo. *BELOW:* The westbound *San Juan* crosses Cat Creek on a snowy December 30, 1948. *BELOW RIGHT:* On Memorial Day weekend in 1952, the homeward-bound Rocky Mountain Railroad Club excursion pauses for water and some oil on the valve gear of the 488.

Robert F. Collins

John Krause

Ross Grenard

103

The depot at Dulce, the first station over the line into New Mexico, has become familiar to modelers through the medium of Timberline Model's HO scale reproduction of the building. It was perhaps best remembered by those who rode the *San Juan* as the stop where the parlor car porter sold ice cream cones to the Jicarilla Apache children as mail for the reservation and the surrounding area was unloaded. *LEFT:* By 1963 the station was closed and boarded up and a new generation had grown up unaware of the delicacies dispensed by the last narrow gauge luxury train, but during the spring and fall, excursions polished the rails and awakened the memories of bygone days.

While the D&RGW was never as essentially bi-lingual as the Quebec Central, it was necessary for the narrow gauge to accomodate the large number of Hispanic citizens who lived along the line and the many who were employed by the railroad, and this was partly accomplished by signs lettered in both Spanish and English. *BELOW:* Near Lumberton, the 490 and a passenger special pass such a sign in an area largely denuded of trees by the early lumbermen who followed the construction of the railroad in the 1880's.

Ross Grenard

Philip R. Hastings

John Krause

Monero was principally noted on the Alamosa Division for two things: having the sharpest curve between Alamosa and Durango, and as the principal source of locomotive coal for that part of the system. The 24 degree curve may be seen in the foreground, and the 492 is preparing to pick up a few gons of the fuel which sustained not only the narrow gauge Mikes, but the standard gauge power at Alamosa as well. Monero was basically a lonely place on a dirt back road and is remembered well by the photographer, for it was here that he first came in contact with the Penitentes, a Spanish religious group of clandestine habits dating back to the Inquisition, and was almost invited, at shotgun-point, to their Holy Week celebration.

Philip R. Hastings

Chama

Chama is the metropolis of this area of northern New Mexico and served as the division point on the line. Located at the foot of Cumbres Pass, it boasted a roundhouse, served as headquarters for the rotary plow, and was on most occasions an eminently worthwhile place to watch trains. Chama was not so large a community that one could become totally divorced from railroad activity. Since the main street parallelled the tracks closely and sat almost on top of the engine terminal, one could easily keep an eye on the activity, even while sipping coffee. *LEFT:* In this case, the 473 awaits the arrival of the *San Juan,* while the 497 will probably follow the passenger train west on a freight. Note particularly the neatly trimmed coal piles, which will come in handy on the 1.42% grades which lie between the waters of the Chama and the Animas. It was standard procedure during the winter to assign a heavier 480 to the train out of Alamosa, in case any drifts should be encountered on Cumbres requiring additional tractive effort. At Chama, the lighter Sports Models would take over for the relatively snow free run to Durango.

John Krause

Robert F. Collins

ABOVE RIGHT: On December 30, 1948, the *San Juan* prepared to leave town after the 473 had been serviced, and her fireman contemplated the comparatively uncluttered yards. The 473's pilot plow indicates that Cumbres is beginning to receive the first harbinger of the long, intense, and harrowing winter of 1949.

BELOW RIGHT: Six and a half years later, 499 arrives from the west with a Rocky Mountain special and finds the yards filled with traffic generated by the oil and gas drilling further west. In a moment, the capacity crowd will disembark and variously head for Kelly's store, the Shamrock Hotel, or the roundhouse, depending on their desire for food, refreshments, or photographs. Soon, another Mike will couple on to the train to lend assistance on the climb up the 4% grade to Cumbres Pass.

Philip R. Hastings
John Krause

The Chama engine terminal consisted of a three-stall roundhouse, and coal, water, and sand facilities. *LEFT:* Under normal circumstances, locomotives were spotted outside between runs, as seen here in the summer of 1954. When the 2-8-2's arrived on the scene, the earlier turntable was abandoned, the pit filled in, and switch leads installed. *ABOVE:* Engines were turned on a wye track west of town, seen here on a wintery April morning in 1953. As the hostler opens the switch, the engines are flanked symbolically by the sawmill and the stockyards: visible symbols of the two sources of traffic which helped support the line for so long.

Just east of Chama began the fifteen and a half miles of 4% grade which continued to Cumbres Pass. Most of the time there was only one train on the railroad, making meets a rare occurrence. ABOVE: In 1954, however, the Rocky Mountain Railroad Club's Memorial Day excursion met a Cumbres turn at Lobato, six miles east of Chama. More normal dispatching procedure would have been to hold the freight at Chama until after the passenger special's arrival there, but for those crowding the platforms, windows, and every available opening, the meet a few miles up the line may have been a whole lot more memorable. ABOVE RIGHT: A few months later, the 492 was caught rolling downgrade, returning from a Cumbres turn job, at a grade crossing outside of Chama. The triangular sign just before the crossing is a warning to flanger operators to raise the blade lest they tear up the crossing. Since cabooses were never turned at the summit of Cumbres, the markers are the reverse of what they should be.

RIGHT: Lobato means "little wolf" in Spanish, and it is here that the rails cross Wolf Creek on the Alamosa-Durango line's second highest trestle. In August of 1949, the 478 brought the westbound *San Juan* across Lobato trestle, drifting along in the splendor of Pullman Green coaches.

Ross Grenard

John Krause

Normal operating procedure out of Chama east called for Alamosa crews to spend two days returning to their home terminal. On the first day, two turns would be operated up to Cumbres Pass and the accumulated cars left at the top of the hill. On the second day, two more turns would be operated; after the fourth trip, the cars would be assembled into a 60 or 70 car freight for the downhill trip to Alamosa. Since the turns averaged 10 to 20 cars at a time, the process generally worked out quite well. The only exception to this was stock trains, which generally went up the hill behind three engines in two sections, in order to get over the road and into Alamosa before the expiration of the 16 hour time limit for stock in transit. On these pages, some of the varied aspects of the Cumbres turns are shown.

LEFT: In this view, the helper is running in the mid-train position near Lobato, due to the large number of empty pipe cars in the consist. While the pipe business did more than anything else to keep the line operating, it did create numerous train handling problems, particularly with empty cars. Faced with a shortage of flats to handle the pipe, and not wanting to buy new cars, the Rio Grande got around the problem by cutting down old box and stock cars no longer needed. But their age and construction would not withstand any rough handling. The problem was eventually solved by rebuilding standard gauge Rio Grande and Western Pacific flat cars to narrow gauge configurations.

BELOW: Crude oil was another commodity moved over Cumbres in volume, and here the 498 leads an early spring turn with the helper properly placed at the rear of the train. The winter of 1954 was a comparatively mild one, and by April the road was open to Cumbres, making possible near winter photography for the first time in memory.

John Krause

John Krause

John Krause

ABOVE: In August of 1952, the 473 was pushing on an eastbound cut of oil cars, properly cut in ahead of the caboose. Since all the narrow gauge cabooses had wooden underframes, cutting in a pusher behind them was expressly forbidden. As a general rule, K-28's were used strictly out of Durango during the 1950's, working east of Chama only when on their way to the shops at Alamosa. The assault on Cumbres reaches its climax at Windy Point, where the tracks curve around an outcropping of volcanic rock on a shelf above the valley, climbing 262 feet in a mile and a half. Always a popular place for photographs, it was a most impressive place to catch an excursion train spread out against the barren rocks as John Krause did in 1954. *RIGHT:* The 492 and 487 lead a melange of differently painted coaches, cabooses, and a refrigerator car for carrying hand baggage around the last curve, about to whistle for the yard limit at Cumbres.

Ross Grenard

The station at Cumbres served the Rio Grande for over a half-century before being bulldozed down in an economy move of dubious rationale. The tidy little building at one time housed the operator and his family, and even after it was closed, was utilized as a shelter by section men and train crews during the snow crises which occurred from time to time. *ABOVE LEFT:* A panorama of Cumbres in May of 1952, shortly after the westbound Rocky Mountain Railroad Club special arrived, powered by the 488. *BELOW, FAR LEFT:* It's April of 1953 and there's still plenty of snow on the ground at Cumbres. The 492 has cut off the train of pipe flats and gons, and turned on the snowshed covered wye. Shortly the road engine will pull the train and caboose 0503 ahead to set off the cars, clearing the west wye switch for the 492 to come out. The cars set out, both engines and the hack will return to Chama. *BELOW LEFT:* Its 5:02 PM on an October afternoon in 1949, and the eastbound *San Juan*, right on the advertised, is paused at Cumbres. There's plenty of time to chat and look around, for a standing air brake test must be made before leaving Cumbres and heading down the 50 miles of 1.42% grade to Antonito. The eastern slope of Cumbres Pass is characterized by sweeping curves whose intent was to crisscross the slopes and push forward without exceeding a maximum of 1.42% grade that a more direct approach would have required. Popular legend holds that one part of the line was laid out by following a drunken burro, yet the tactics employed between Antonito and Cumbres have been used successfully in the construction of every other low grade railroad in the U.S. Just east of Cumbres, Tanglefoot Curve or Cumbres Loop offers an excellent example of this type of engineering. *BELOW:* An eastbound freight creeps around the loops preceeded by the helper engine. As a rule, two Alamosa crews would work to Chama: a full train crew and an engine crew for the helper. Returning from Chama, the helper crew ran ahead light, for this earned a lower rate of pay than having them run attached to the freight, and served the additional purpose of acting as a pilot of sorts for the descending freight.

RIGHT: This view looks in the same direction, but the photographer was down off the hill and standing on the passing track at the highest level. From this lower perspective the rise of the track is more apparent as a westbound fan trip ascends the Loop towards Cumbres. One more complete 180° turn is to be made before the loops are negotiated. The perspective makes the curves look a great deal sharper than the actual 20-degree maximum.

John Krause

John Krause

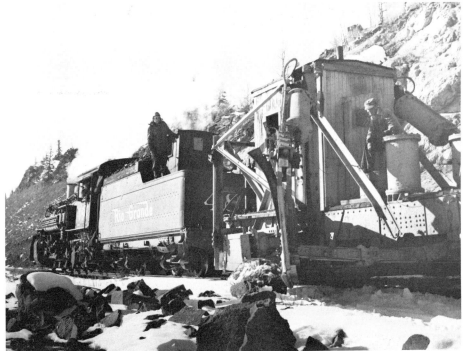

At Osier, approximately 13 miles east of Cumbres, the railroad describes another major loop and starts into Toltec Gorge. Osier is principally known for its inaccesability and as a spot where a great deal of snow drifting always occurred. *LEFT:* On a spring day in 1955, the 488 brings an eastbound down the hill in a sweeping vista which shows the potential of the area for drifting. In addition to the water tank and section house, Osier also had a cache of coal for snow emergencies, intended primarily for flanger train engines or rotary plows.

FAR LEFT: A view from the cab of the 484 looking back towards Toltec, as a flanger extra clears the line in January of 1963. The snow was not yet deep enough to call out the rotary as had been done the previous year, but prudent operating policy dictated that the fallen snow be cleared before it had a chance to freeze to ice.

BELOW LEFT: "Watch out for rocks where liable to fall" is a standard phrase appearing on Rio Grande train orders during the winter and spring on both the standard and narrow gauge lines, and this photo shows why. Boulders such as these can derail trains, cause bodily injury, and complicate operations greatly. In this case, the flanger wing is being used to push such a piece of granite away from the track to insure that it doesn't foul a passing freight.

The Rock Tunnel at Toltec has been a popular spot to stop and view the gorge from the enclosed area along the stone fill. It is here that the Garfield Memorial is located, on the spot where an impromptu service was held by an excursion party on learning of the assassination in 1881. In later years, it was a popular photo stop on the numerous excursions over the narrow gauge. *RIGHT:* The 480 comes storming out of the tunnel in a scene illustrating the stark, rocky, and precipitous nature of Toltec Gorge.

Between Chama and Antonito, the track swings back and forth between Colorado and New Mexico a number of times. In fact, well into the late 1940's the area was so remote and uncharted that even the railroad itself was not sure at some points whether their track was in one state or the other; the advent of aerial surveys in the 1950's finally resolved the question. Above Sublette, the line climbs steadily through the pines and volcanic rocks, looping around curves and climbing perceptibly out of the sagebrush towards Toltec. BELOW: In 1939, Bob Collins rode the westbound *San Juan* and snapped it blasting around one of the many curves with an impressive head end consist and the 473 on the point.

Robert F. Collins

Robert F. Collins

Antonito

Ross Grenard   John Krause

ABOVE LEFT: A flanger train heads west a few miles out of Antonito in a scene in which the railroad represents the only evidence of man's intrusion into the area. It is interesting that much of the snow trouble that afflicted the narrow gauge occurred in the area immediately west of Antonito, where the combination of vast, open spaces, devoid of anything to break up the fury of a winter storm, and the tendency of the volcanic pumice to impact itself into drifted snow created problems all out of proportion to the climate and topography of the area. *BELOW, FAR LEFT:* The 481 pauses near the coal dock after bringing a standard gauge freight down from Alamosa. The idler car directly behind the engine effected the coupling between the narrow gauge Mike and the standard gauge cars. *BELOW LEFT:* The 499 heads west out of Antonito with a fan trip in 1955, past the stone depot. Behind the depot can be seen the track which once headed south to Santa Fe, New Mexico on the fabled Chili Line; the coal dock and water tank lie in the distance. Antonito and Alamosa are connected by 28 miles of tangent track which was principally noted for its mixed gauge operations, made possible by idler cars and three rail track. The line is relatively flat, curveless, and gave the engineers an opportunity to open up their charges a bit after the 20 and 25 mph maximums found on the other parts of the narrow gauge. Prior to 1951, the *San Juan* was a regular morning and evening event along this stretch, and in most cases the residents of the San Luis Valley were able to set their watches by its passage. *ABOVE RIGHT:* At precisely 7:31 AM on the morning of July 3, 1948, the 476 rolled Train 215 away from a station stop at La Jara in the glory of its green livery, clattering across the mixed gauge switches enroute to Toltec, Cumbres, Chama, and Durango.

BELOW RIGHT: Seven years later, the 1955 Rocky Mountain Railroad Club excursion heads down the last lap into Alamosa trailed by office car B-7, the last narrow gauge passenger equipment to wear the traditional Pullman Green. As the 499 rolls along across the sagebrush, the passengers mull over the memories of three days on the narrow gauge, and a group takes the air on the back platform in a properly plutocratic manner. The group includes Robert LeMassena, the definitive chronicler of the Rio Grande, at the left of the platform, his wife directly ahead and the author at their side.

Ross Grenard

John Krause

During the years prior to the demise of the narrow gauge, Antonito turns were operated with a variety of power, including narrow gauge 2-8-2's, diesel yard switchers, and EMD Geeps of various types. Best remembered are the standard gauge C-48 class 2-8-0's, which for decades performed admirably around the Rio Grande as switchers, road engines, and even on occasion as passenger power. Their last stand was made at Alamosa, and in October of 1955 *(LEFT)*, John Treen caught one of the last of the breed rolling west out of Alamosa with a mixed consist. The primary mission of such operations was to set out and pick up these cars at communities along the way. The 1167 has less than a year of service left, but she rolls along with great authority past the Coors billboard in the bright sunlight of a San Luis Valley afternoon.

BELOW LEFT: Alamosa was the first home for the equipment collection which became the nucleus of the Colorado Railroad Museum at Golden. That there remains anything of a tangible nature to remind Coloradoans of their narrow gauge heritage is due in no small part to the activities at the old Alamosa museum and motel and to Robert W. Richardson in particular, who realized the necessity to preserve both the hardware and the fleeting pictorial image of the institution to which the Centennial state owes so much. On Memorial Day of 1954, the 487 brought a homeward bound excursion by the building which served as the museum at the time. Soon the last curve into Alamosa will be rounded, the train will ease into the station, and the 300 passengers will head for home, each with their own special memories of the wonders of the narrow-gauge.

BELOW: Since cabooses at Alamosa were assigned to individual conductors, the luck of the call would sometimes result in a narrow gauge hack being used on an otherwise standard gauge train, with standard gauge idler cars being used to make the hitch.

John Krause

John L. Treen

John L. Treen

Alamosa

At Alamosa were located the shops which maintained the locomotives and cars for the narrow gauge, as well as transfer facilities for all types of equipment, and a roundhouse which, until 1956, serviced both standard and narrow gauge locomotives. *RIGHT:* In April of 1953, Phil Hastings recorded the engine terminal as the 492 and 499 moved out to power a Chama bound freight. In the background can be discerned the oil refinery which was the consignee of the crude oil lugged over Cumbres in Gramps tankers. The turntable leads to the standard gauge roundhouse at the left from which protrudes the tender of a 2-10-2, and the narrow gauge roundhouse on the right; further to the right are the shop buildings. The string of passenger cars in the left foreground wait patiently for the beginning of the Silverton operations in June.

Philip R. Hastings

LEFT: The yards and terminal at Alamosa had their moments of calm, and here one of the durable and capable 1100 class Consolidations sits between switching chores as the narrow and standard gauge cars intermingle and the essential geometry of the dual gauge trackage and the steam era facilities pose in solitude, awaiting the pipe traffic rush which was to descend upon Alamosa in the next two years.

ABOVE: The Alamosa station dated from 1906, and was an impressive structure containing both passenger facilities and the offices of the Division Superintendent and the dispatcher. By 1953, when this photo was taken, the Alamosa Division had been absorbed into the Pueblo Division, and the only passenger service, Trains 15 and 16 to Pueblo, would soon come to an end. The great days of through Pullmans, transfer of mail and express, and of the passenger business in general are over, and only one soul seems to show any interest as the two K-37's stop to pick up their orders. Since operation of the narrow gauge was directed at this time by John C. Kennefick, later president of the Union Pacific and patron of the renowned 8444, we may wonder if he was looking down upon this scene from his office in the station.

Rosters

The equipment of the narrow gauge was varied and individualistic in many cases, and reflected the effects of numerous rebuilding programs along the way. The Rio Grande Southern equipment in particular, was almost all purchased secondhand, and numbered several one of a kind rarities to further intrigue the aficionado or student of rare items. Since formal rosters have either been published or are in preparation, the purpose of this section is to show a few of the more interesting pieces of equipment.

Both the 312 (ABOVE) and the 272 (BELOW) were built as open-platform coaches and with six other cars, were rebuilt in a 1937 program for use on the *Shavano* and *San Juan*. During the rebuilding, vestibules replaced open platforms, modern plumbing was added, reclining seats replaced red plush, and electric lights supplanted the kerosene coach lamps. In 1957, to increase the seating capacity for Silverton service, the 2-1 recliners were removed and ex-Denver trolley coach seats were installed.

Ross Grenard

Robert F. Collins

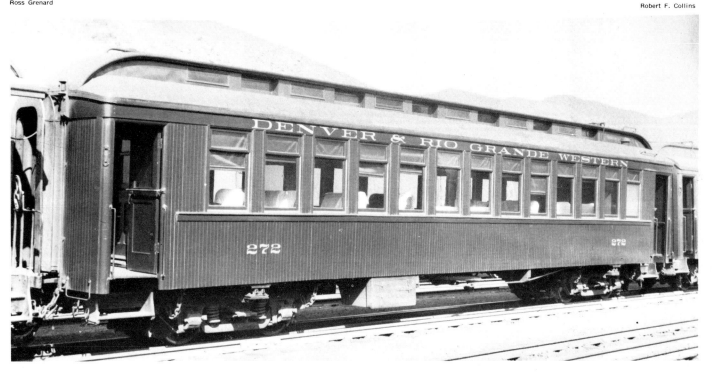

Ross Grenard

Robert F. Collins

The parlor car *Chama* was rebuilt from a coach in 1937, equipped with dining table and galley, and was used on the *San Juan* trains until their demise. Unlike the straight parlor car *Salida (BELOW)*, which carried the markers on the *Shavano*, the three *San Juan* parlors did not have an enclosed platform. Both *Salida* and *Chama* have long departed from Colorado. The *Salida* was sold to the Nacionales de Mexico in 1941, and is probably no longer in service, while the *Chama* along with the sister parlor *Durango* and two coaches were sold ten years later to Knott's Berry Farm, where they operate in company with two 1881 2-8-0's and K-27 class Mudhen No. 464. The three *San Juan* parlors, *Alamosa*, *Durango*, and *Chama*, constituted the highest form of luxury available to the general public in the latter years of passenger operation, and these two photos *(RIGHT)* illustrate what the $ 3.00 step-up charge would purchase in the way of amenities. The buffet operation was, through most of its existence, the only Rio Grande diner to actually *make* money, and its steward was generally amenable to letting the passengers furnish their own steaks, generally purchased at Durango, and would even chill and serve wine if it was desired.

Phil Ronfor photographed the *Alamosa's* interior in September of 1950, as the Jackson & Sharp product rounded out seven decades of service on the narrow gauge that had begun as Horton Chair Car No. 25. The sole parlor car retained by the railroad, it was used as an office car and on excursions for six years until it was converted into a coach. Renovated early this year, it will no doubt round out a century of service, a record any Amfleet or Superliner equipment will be very hard put to duplicate.

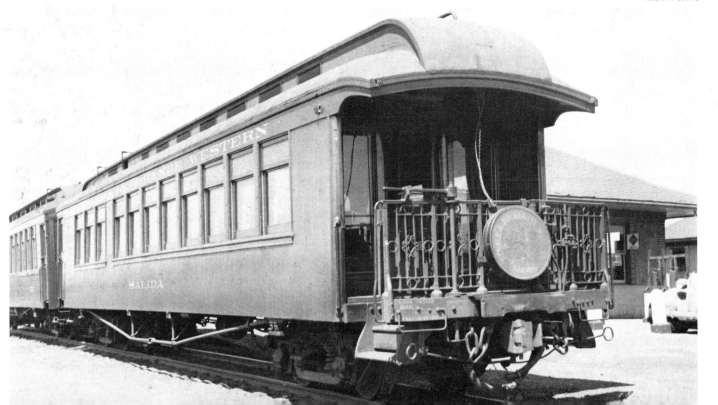

Philip A. Ronfor

Philip A. Ronfor

Robert F. Collins

Ross Grenard

The carriage of the United States Mail was an important aspect of the narrow-gauge passenger operations, and it is not incidental to note that the *San Juan* was considered of such importance to the Post Office that the Rio Grande was offered a considerable increase in mail revenue to keep the train running. In any event, narrow gauge RPO cars were fascinating pieces of equipment, and their cancellations are highly prized souvenirs of the days when Herodotus' words ("Neither rain nor snow nor gloom of night...") were implemented by plow-fronted K-27's and steel hearted RPO clerks riding in wooden mail cars.

LEFT AND BELOW: The right and left sides of a standard Rio Grande Railway Post Office car are illustrated. Note the varying window configuration from side to side, and the lack of any passageway from the other cars. In the photo of 122, at the extreme right on the adjacent car, some of the equipment for the generator units used to supply power for the electrically-lighted cars can be seen. On the roofs the conduits for the electrical wiring are visible. After the termination of the *San Juan*, the RPO cars were converted to maintenance of way service, and used as bunk, tool, and cook cars for the rotaries. In some instances, end platforms were added for easy access and the side doors sealed off. *ABOVE RIGHT:* The 053 is an ex-RPO converted to camp car service. *BELOW RIGHT:* Combination car 212 was constructed in 1882, and was used all over the narrow gauge prior to assignment on the Silverton Branch. In addition to making the last run on the Pagosa Springs Branch in 1934, it appeared in the movies *Ticket to Tomahawk* and *Denver & Rio Grande* and survives today as a coach with a stand-up snack bar in what was once the baggage section.

The RGS Business Car B-20 *(BELOW, FAR RIGHT)* was built in 1881 by Jackson & Sharp as Rio Grande Car A, at a cost of $ 5,000, and became Otto Mears' private car *San Juan* in 1890. Renamed *Edna* in 1909, it was used sporadically over the years for official purposes and was sold to Knott's Berry Farm in 1951. In 1949, it was repainted by volunteers from the Rocky Mountain Railroad Club for use on the 1949 excursion, and is seen here near Lizard Head.

Ross Grenard   Robert F. Collins   Ross Grenard

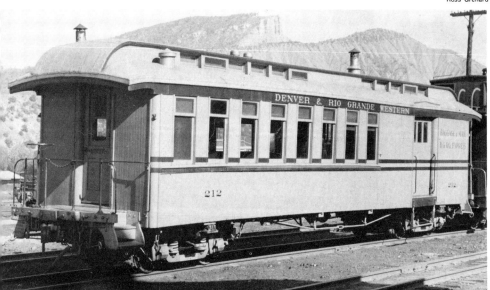

Sam Fredericks

Sam Fredericks

ABOVE LEFT: RGS 2101 was built in 1909 for the Colorado & Southern and was one of three reefers purchased in 1938 by Victor Miller to handle perishable traffic. The cars were equipped with Bettendorf cast steel trucks, steel underframes, and were considerably more modern than their Rio Grande counterparts. While many of the Victor Miller cars were sold in a short time to the Chicago Freight Car Parts Co. for use on narrow gauge lines in Alaska and Oahu during World War II, the 2101 remained on the property to the end, and was the only reefer left on the roster.

ABOVE RIGHT: No selection of narrow gauge equipment would be complete without a photo of one of the double deck stock cars so popular for shipping sheep to market. The 5564 was constructed in 1904 and was photographed in 1939 by Sam Fredericks before the speed-line Rio Grande lettering was added to the right side of the cars.

BELOW LEFT: Caboose 0500 was the first car of the group designed to withstand the stresses of pusher operation on Marshall Pass. Originally built as a four-wheel

model, it was later fitted with eight wheels. Since train crews always bunked in their cabooses when on jobs that required rest time, 0500 and its sisters were used mostly in later years for short runs or to carry section hands on flanger and snow plow runs, for they lack adequate sleeping accomodations. Most were stricken from the roster in the early 1950's, and 0500 was sold to the old Narrow Gauge Museum and Motel at Alamosa at that time.

BELOW RIGHT: RGS 0403 was built by the Rio Grande for the RGS in 1891, and was one of the few pieces of equipment the RGS ever owned. It is shown here at Ridgway in 1947, lettered in the old manner and ready to leave on the tail of an excursion train. The plate on the lower center portion of the siding declares, "Defense Supplies Corporation, Washington, D.C., Owner and Lessor", a leftover from the period when the Federal agency purchased the railroad's facilities and equipment and leased them back to the receiver for $ 1,000 per month plus interest.

Sam Fredericks

Philip A. Ronfor

RIGHT: Goose No. 4 was constructed in May 1932, and after the abandonment was placed on display at Telluride. Along the way it received a Wayne bus body, but in 1939 it still looked very much like a Pierce-Arrow when Sam Fredericks photographed it at Dolores.

BELOW: Work Goose No. 6 was constructed by Ridgway shops in 1934 to replace steam work trains, and incorporated in its makeup some of the spare parts from the dismantled Goose No. 1. It was generally driven by the roadmaster and served the RGS until the end. Bob Collins caught the Goose at Rico on May 31, 1949, flying the white flags of an extra.

BELOW RIGHT: The second No. 25 was working out her last days in service at Rico in 1939. The 1899 Schenectady product was dismantled in 1940, after a career which included service on both the Florence & Cripple Creek and the RGS. Her tender was transferred to sister engine 20, and survives with that engine in honorable retirement at the Colorado Railroad Museum at Golden.

Robert W. Andrews

Sam Fredericks

Robert F. Collins

Sam Fredericks

ABOVE LEFT: The 461 was still a Rio Grande engine in 1939, when it awaited assignment at Montrose. *CENTER LEFT:* The 479 served as the regular power for the *Shavano* during its last years, and went to Alaska in 1942 after receiving a form of Greetings from Uncle Sam. *BELOW LEFT:* The 271 served out its final years as the Durango switcher and the 1882 Baldwin C-16 class consolidation was sold to Montezuma Lumber in 1941. *BELOW RIGHT:* Largest, heaviest, and most powerful of all narrow gauge 2-8-0's, the 375 was built by Baldwin in 1904 and came to the Rio Grande in 1916 from the Crystal River Railroad along with her two smaller sisters, 360 and 361. Developing almost as much tractive effort as a Mudhen, the 375 held down the Silverton Branch job for many years and was scrapped in 1949. It was the sole occupant of the C-25 class, the only one-engine class on the road. *CENTER RIGHT:* No. 41, a Baldwin product of 1881, served the Rio Grande until it was purchased by the RGS in 1916. After the abandonment, the 2-8-0 was sold along with Goose No. 3 to Knott's Berry Farm in California.

Sam Fredericks

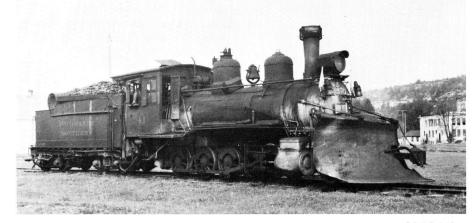

Robert F. Collins

Sam Fredericks

Sam Fredericks

CENTER LEFT: Constructed by Baldwin in 1925, the 486 saw service out of both Salida and Alamosa. With canvas waterbag properly hung on the cab side to stay cool, she awaited a call at Chama in 1949.

BELOW LEFT: The 360 and 361 came from the coal hauling Crystal River Railroad and developed a respectable 21,000 lbs. of tractive effort. Much of their career was spent at Gunnison, as they were the heaviest power that could be operated through the Black Cañon. Their outside frames earned them the name "Little Mudhens", and their good looks the admiration of railfans and modelers. Bob Collins caught the 360 at Montrose preparing for a return trip over Cerro Summit in 1939.

BELOW RIGHT: The last engines acquired for the narrow gauge were also the most powerful, having been converted from standard gauge 2-8-0's at the Burnham shops in Denver in 1928 and 1930. The 497, seen here in pre-speed line days, had almost three decades of service ahead of her yet when Bob Collins shot her at Salida in August of 1939, and was to be an active participant in the last steam operation in North America. Since the steam locomotive is considered to be a most human and intuitive machine, one may wonder if the 497 is somehow not aware of this fact.

CENTER RIGHT: Next to the last of the once numerous C-16 Consolidations, the 278 was a sprightly septegenerian when she posed for Phil Ronfor in 1952. Admired by fans from coast to coast, the engine was given to the citizens of Montrose for display, but now has been acquired by the National Park Service and is on display near Cimmaron.

ABOVE RIGHT: RGS No. 42 was using a borrowed Rio Grande tender at Durango in 1949, as it awaited a call to serve as a plow engine, a helper, or on a stock train. The 1887 Baldwin went to the RGS in 1916, and had the distinction of being the last of that road's engines in steam.

Ross Grenard

Philip A. Ronfor

Ross Grenard

Robert F. Collins

Robert F. Collins

With curtains drawn, Rio Grande Southern Goose No. 5 stands at Ridgway waiting transportation to a museum. Her journeys on the narrow gauge circle are over. Except for a few tourist operations, the narrow gauge and its famed circle are gone. In the jet airplane and diesel truck age, there just isn't any more need for Colorado's little trains. Its our hope they'll continue to run forever in *Colorado Memories*.

John Krause &
Ross Grenard

Tom Gilbert

Narrow gauge equipment is on display at a number of places in Colorado, including the Colorado Railroad Museum at Golden. Portions of the old narrow gauge circle can still be ridden on the Denver & Rio Grande Western from Durango to Silverton, and over the Cumbres & Toltec Scenic Railroad from Chama to Antonito. Other short stretches of narrow gauge are to be found in other parts of the state, along with locomotives and cars on display. We do not list them here since such displays are all too often subject to moving and change. Check up to date directories, Colorado travel folders, and other available literature including *Railfan Magazine* before starting your trip to narrow gauge circle country.